PENGUIN BOOKS

BOLLYWOOD NATION

Vamsee Juluri was born in Hyderabad in 1969 and is a professor of media studies at the University of San Francisco. His books include *Becoming a Global Audience: Longing and Belonging in Indian Music Television* and the novel *The Mythologist*.

BOLLYWOOD
NATION

India through Its Cinema

VAMSEE JULURI

PENGUIN BOOKS

PENGUIN BOOKS
Published by the Penguin Group
Penguin Books India Pvt Ltd, 11 Community Centre, Panchsheel Park, New Delhi
110 017, India
Penguin Group (USA) Inc., 375 Hudson Street, New York, New York 10014, USA
Penguin Group (Canada), 90 Eglinton Avenue East, Suite 700, Toronto, Ontario,
M4P 2Y3, Canada (a division of Pearson Penguin Canada Inc.)
Penguin Books Ltd, 80 Strand, London WC2R 0RL, England
Penguin Ireland, 25 St Stephen's Green, Dublin 2, Ireland (a division of Penguin Books Ltd)
Penguin Group (Australia), 707 Collins Street, Melbourne, Victoria 3008, Australia
(a division of Pearson Australia Group Pty Ltd)
Penguin Group (NZ), 67 Apollo Drive, Rosedale, Auckland 0632, New Zealand
(a division of Pearson New Zealand Ltd)
Penguin Books (South Africa) (Pty) Ltd, Block D, Rosebank Office Park, 181 Jan Smuts
Avenue, Parktown North, Johannesburg 2193, South Africa

Penguin Books Ltd, Registered Offices: 80 Strand, London WC2R 0RL, England

First published by Penguin Books India 2013

The views and opinions expressed in this book are the author's own and the facts are as
reported by him which have been verified to the extent possible, and the publishers are not
in any way liable for the same.

ISBN 9780143065111

For sale in the Indian Subcontinent, Singapore and Malaysia only

Typeset in Sabon Roman by SÜRYA, New Delhi
Printed at HT Media Ltd

For my parents,
JVR and JJ,
God, Country, Home and World.

And for WS,
Life.

'. . . so long as Hindi films are watched and their songs sung, India will survive.'

—Ramachandra Guha, *India after Gandhi*

CONTENTS

Foreword   xi

INTRODUCTION   1

1. GOD

   God as One (and Many)   19
   God as One of Us   24
   God as Good   30
   God, Devotion, Real Life   38

2. COUNTRY

   Imagined India   56
   Mother (1930s–50s)   61
   Motherland (1950s–60s)   65
   Land (1970s)   74
   Realism and Recognition   82

3. HOME

   The Political and Economic Roots of Home   92
   Home Comforts: The Rise of Doordarshan   96
   Home Pride: NTR   104

Homelands: *Ramayan*   114
No Direction?   128

4. WORLD

India and the World: From Independence to   135
    Liberalization
The Whole World is *Baywatch*ing   140
Made in India   147
Friends, Families and Foreign Locations   154
Vigilantes, Terrorists, Gangsters   166
'Global and Medieval', but Gandhian Still?   174

AFTERWORD: LIFE   183

Acknowledgements   197
References   201
Index   207

FOREWORD

THE FIRST SCENE IN INDIA'S FIRST FILM IS ABOUT A MOTHER. DADASAHEB Phalke's *Raja Harischandra* (1913) begins with a rather tranquil, everyday scene of a queen doting over her son as his father, the king, teaches him archery. As I watched this film one monsoon afternoon at the National Film Archives in Pune a few years ago, I felt overwhelmed by what it all meant, by the world that it had inaugurated. I felt worshipful, and I can only explain the origins of that reverence so much. It was perhaps the knowledge that this was something rare, precious, the work of the man we call the 'Father of Indian Cinema'. It was perhaps the sort of reverence Indians feel for works of art and literature, a 'Saraswati Maa' moment, as it were, or perhaps it was the reverence we feel for elders, for the past, for a sense of heritage and where we have come from. In my case, that reverence was much closer—personal, one might say, but I prefer existential. My work, my professional identity, my sense of intellect and value, all come from that world that Phalke began. To put it in plainer terms, my bread and butter, so to speak, comes from that world too, and I feel grateful. But my debt to cinema goes even deeper than that. There is a reason, perhaps, why I noticed that the first scene in the first film made in India is about a mother. My mother happens to be a film star. So, to embark on a book about a national cinema that began with a scene about a mother, I cannot begin with anyone other than my mother. My book and my existence have a lot to do with her, and the fact of her having been a film star. Her name is Jamuna. She has acted in nearly two hundred films in four languages and has received many awards, accolades and titles. The one I admire most is 'Prajanati', the People's Actress.

The earliest memories I have of everything in the world seem to revolve around my mother's stardom—the people, the activity, the studios, the press and the posters. And, most of all, the fans and the wild adulation they all seemed to show her. I remember frenzied hands, autograph books, happy faces, screams, whistles, madness, chaos that could come upon us out of nowhere. I remember the slightly more civil flow, like a waterfall of admiration, of shiny, tonsured fans walking down the driveway to our house for her darshan in the morning. I remember the actual process of shooting on some occasions too, slow, painful, bright, hot, endlessly repetitive. I remember the people who made up the production of her world—companions, managers, make-up people, tailors, relatives, drivers, aspiring writers, sometimes even runaway kids who showed up at our home in search of a role and somehow now had to be returned safely. All of this made me realize very early in my life perhaps that cinema was clearly something very, very important. It was not just something that I read about, or even talked about, very much though. In my family—for all the incursions the world of films may have made into our sense of self and reality for generations to come—cinema, and especially Indian cinema, was deemed unsuitable for children. To some extent, this was not uncommon for the times. My parents were worried parents, first and last. *The Sound of Music* and *Hatari* were perhaps the only films they took me to see, of their own accord. All else was negotiated—Charles Bronson, *The Dirty Dozen* and, in time, the James Bond films. The impediments to watching films of course were many. They were so special that they demanded sacrifice in anticipation, like trying to sleep the whole afternoon to rest the eyes so the evening's show wouldn't harm them. Eyesight and homework were the chief concerns of my parents—and I suppose all parents in general—at the time.

Then, there was the whole angle of how film-watching, such as it was permitted, every two or three months, had to be confined to English titles. No one really explained the logic to me. For my father, it was virtually unthinkable to watch Hindi or Telugu films. For my mother, it could be negotiated, but very rarely. She took me to watch *Sholay* at Hyderabad's Ramakrishna theatre in 1975. It was dark, and we entered late. We sat in a box, thanks to one of NTR's sons, who was there at the time. A few years later, my mother took me to see *Don*, once again, ironically, in another theatre owned by NTR. We went out during the interval to the manager's office, where one of his sons chatted with us, and then we waited out a swimsuit-and-poolside scene in the film, too, over there. Apart from these concessions to the towering heroics of Amitabh Bachchan, there was not much by way of domestic film-watching, even with my mother. I saw some of her films from time to time. In fact, the first time was in 1978, when a retrospective of her work was screened to celebrate her silver jubilee in cinema—quite a grand, stadium-sized event in itself. The old, black-and-white films of hers—the Golden Age everyone now adores—were delightful. I briefly began to profess my great admiration for NTR, even though somehow it wasn't commonly done in school, which was perhaps a bit too cosmopolitan in those days for local culture. Once, when my parents were both out of town, I persuaded my cook and my neighbour's driver to take us to see his 70-mm blockbuster entitled *A Man Like Fire* or something like that. It was a terribly decrepit theatre, and there was some really desperate problem that arose which had everyone around me worried, though I don't know what. Years later, I blew off an exam to watch a screening of what would be one of my mother's last films, the Hindi historical fantasy *Raj Tilak*. I was severely reprimanded for that, too. But I had to, for I had previously watched the film being filmed, in Bombay's famous R.K. Studios at that.

Now I cannot ever say if my parents would have been less discouraging of my watching films if they knew that one day this would become my career. In fact, the whole source of their concern seems to have been *that*—not just that films were bad for the eyesight and studies, but that I might decide to demand that I make them my career. If I did that, the loss, of course, would not be merely for the better career I ought to have picked—like doctor or engineer—but, really, for my humanity itself. The industry, to put it simply, was feared. It could easily do in ordinary people. That I had to resist all temptation even to contemplate it was imprinted on me meticulously by my parents. It was awkward, because fans and friends invariably asked if I wanted to be a film star when I grew up. Since it seemed unthinkable, I didn't say it. I didn't even think it. But I must admit that, on the two occasions when there was talk in the house of my acting in a film, once when I was four or five, and again when I was nine, I was tempted. I was incredibly tempted. The first time was the role of Krishna—a walk-on, or perhaps a stand-up-straight-and-be-still part. The second time, it was for the role of the young prince Salim, son to NTR's Akbar and my mother's Jodhabai. For some reason, my mother discussed this idea quite seriously. My father, too, didn't object. It was even mentioned to NTR. But in the end, it fell apart when it was discovered that the part called for the young Salim to sip some wine from his father's regal Mughal goblet. That alarmed my mother, incredibly. She squashed the idea forever. My last shot at acting, next to the great NTR at that, slipped away like the Thums Up or Rasna (which was what I expected to find in the goblet) from a parched child's lips. I grew up with little to do with films, except for my mother's fame. That followed me everywhere, even to America where her fans could be found, unexpectedly, in small Midwestern towns to take care of me and feed me, as I played the starving grad student in real life. The irony, which was almost apparent to me by this time, was that my career, such as I was trying to find one, would end up being about my mother's world, about cinema, and media in general.

I ended up in such a career quite by default, at least in the beginning. After a miserable and unsuccessful attempt to study engineering after high school, I quit in the hope that I would somehow be able to make a living as a writer. I was told—and in time, I understood—that one needed to have something to write about in order to be a writer, that one ought to learn something about the world, or some part of it at least. It was the early 1990s, and India was in the throes of its satellite-television revolution. It all seemed so exciting and intense that I thought I could spend my life writing about the media and, for once, I stuck to that pursuit. I found something I liked to learn about, and I did. And it was in that context—as a graduate student studying the media, living in America, dealing with homesickness in a new land and too many worries about the future of the world as befitted an intellectual in training—that I found, at long last, an experience of meaning, of truth even, in the world of Indian cinema. Maybe it was *Hum Aapke Hain Koun..!*, a film that so moved and puzzled me I conducted an audience research project to learn more about how people saw it, leading to a conference presentation in Finland and my first scholarly publication some time later. Or maybe it was even later, in the lonely and fear-filled days after 9/11 in America when, one evening, I stopped following the crazy paranoid world of American news and put on a tape of *Mooga Manasulu* (*Milan* in Hindi), and found a world of worry slip away from my shoulders at the sound of the first bars of the hit song, 'Godari Gattundi'. It was my mother in there and somehow my world felt better, all at once. Somewhere in the years that followed, I became convinced that there was more to our films than we had really acknowledged, as fans, or as critics. I began using Indian films in my classes, most notably the film *Mission Kashmir* (2000) in a course that talked a great deal about terrorism and violence in the media. I also began to read Gandhi for this course.

In time, over many classes and films and books, a framework of sorts began to appear, which seemed to connect my instinctual appreciation of some of our films with some of the academic theories and studies I was familiar with. It seemed there was a way of seeing the history of India—or at least its popular self-perception—in terms of its films, from the earliest days to the present. It was this way of seeing that I used to structure a special course I taught on India at the University of San Francisco, and subsequent classes on Indian cinema. It is an attempt to tell a story about India, through the stories that our films were telling us. It draws from a critical academic tradition, one in which I was trained, but it is, on the whole, a task of appreciation rather than criticism—political or aesthetic. It is, to put it simply, an attempt to see the best in our films or, at least, the best in us that our films have shown us. It is not entirely academic, for that reason, though it might sound that way. It is a tribute to a way of seeing the world. And maybe, if I have succeeded in echoing some of that sensibility in this book, I will offer that sentiment as a mark of respect, affection, and gratitude to my mother, and to that incredible world she has been such an indelible part of, for me and millions of others in our part of the country at the very least.

There is much I have looked away from; but there is much, again, that I remember with gratitude, especially of how much my mother and her work have brought me to where I am today. I think of the National Film Awards of 1984, when my mother took me along with her to New Delhi, as she served on the jury. I was fifteen and probably shouldn't have been there, but it was one the most memorable experiences of my life. I remember the greats of the world of cinema and criticism, from all over the country at that. The acclaimed Tamil director K. Balachander was there, and many other people whose greatness I probably did not quite grasp yet. But my mother, in her enthusiasm, found for me a friend and mentor for all of the few days I tagged along. She introduced

me to the late critic and writer Iqbal Masud, and told him I
loved books and writing. He was the first person to tell me a
writer needs to read first, and learn about things. He was
patient and chatted with me at length. Then, one day, when a
Telugu film was screened and there was no one to translate, I
offered to do it for him. The Best Picture Award that year
went to G.V. Iyer's *Adi Shankaracharya*. My mother really
supported it, because it was Sanskrit, and the source of our
glorious past. The Best Picture in Telugu went to *Rangula
Kala*—the one I interpreted for Mr Masud—a progressive
art film, if there was one. My mother fought for that one too.
I mention these two films now, nearly thirty years later,
because my mother's choices tell me something of her
intellectual, political and cultural sensibilities under the all
too blinding dazzle of her glamorous celebrity and stardom. I
realize now that, in the public sphere at least, there are not
too many people who might value both these sorts of films—
red and saffron—at the same time. She did, and in some
ways, as will be apparent in this book, I try to do the same
too.

INTRODUCTION

★

A FEW YEARS AGO, I TAUGHT A CLASS AT THE UNIVERSITY OF SAN Francisco called 'Understanding India'. The goal of the class was not simply to presume to understand India as if it were a mere object waiting to be interpreted by the Western academy, but rather to recognize the ways in which India understands its own self. Our interest essentially was in this process of understanding in a broad cultural sense, particularly in relation to the media, and the social and historical circumstances in which it takes place. We explored these concerns first in a semester-long class, reading about religion, history, politics, media and many other subjects. Then, we set out on a six-week-long summer programme based at the serene campus of the University of Hyderabad. My students listened to lectures on a wide range of subjects here, and also visited a number of places to illustrate those classes. We visited the historical sites, like Golconda fort and the great city of Hampi. We saw the shiny Information Technology parks of 'Cyberabad' and the many new malls and restaurants Hyderabad now boasts of. We visited the IMAX theatre complex, where my students noted the presence of 'escalator ushers' to help the masses of unaccustomed visitors to the new conveyance. We also went to the Ramoji Film City, a spectacular studio and entertainment park outside Hyderabad which is waiting, like Hyderabad, like India, to rise and make its mark in the world. Throughout, we returned to the theme of our central question—*How and under what conditions does India understand itself and the world?*

By the time the class ended, I was left with a sense of accomplishment for having brought the two countries I call home together in a small way, but I had to acknowledge to my students that our core question would perhaps always remain slightly rhetorical. How does one dare to summarize how India sees itself and the world in the matter of a few months? As my students often noted, which India are we talking about, in the first place—the cities or the villages; HITEC City or the slums of construction workers around it; the India of the young or the India of everyone? Add to these questions all the other dimensions of diversity in India that we could not even begin to explore in five weeks—region, religion, community, a long list of disparate factors indeed. Underlying these questions of course was the all-important one—What do we mean by India? We live in an age of what some would call postmodern anxieties. In academics, it has become more fashionable to speak of something called 'South Asia' rather than India, because 'India' seems to invoke too many questions. Can we speak of anything any more? Is there really some way we can presume to speak for, or speak about, India as a whole?

Despite these cautionary points, this book is indeed an attempt to represent India, and, as such, is perhaps best served by beginning with a new twist on an old story—that of the elephant and the blind men. A group of blind men, so goes the story, stumble upon an elephant and begin to feel around to try and figure out what it is. Unaware of the 'big picture', the interlocutors in this epistemological adventure call out numerous erroneous 'eurekas'. One man thinks he has found a rope, but it is only the elephant's tail. Another thinks he has stumbled upon a pillar, but it is, in fact, one of the elephant's formidable legs. But none of them realizes that what they have before them is nothing less than an elephant. Now, it may be no surprise if I say that India is like the elephant in this story. But there is one more layer we could add to this tale—What if we find, blindness notwithstanding, that the elephant is saying something? To be precise, the elephant is singing. Even if it seems to be singing in many different languages, it is ultimately singing in one voice, and it is a voice that comes right from the elephant's heart. If India is the elephant in this story, then its cinema is its voice; it carries in it the weight of many experiences and observations, and it hints at a variety of registers in which it expresses itself. It is a voice that changes, as does its history, but it never lacks for one thing—and that is conviction. We may not be able to understand the whole of India in a classroom or in a book, but we can certainly learn much by listening to how India has been speaking, at least through its most popular mass medium.

This book, essentially, is not so much a history of Indian cinema and its stars as much as *a study of India through its cinema*. It looks at what Indian cinema has been saying about the world around it, behind what seems to passing observers as merely a superficial (yet opaque) veil of unending dances, weddings and songs. It is my hope to show in this book that the stories of Indian cinema are not simply entertainment, as fans tend to think they are; nor are they ideological conspiracies to oppress whole groups of people, as academics like me sometimes seem to imply they are. Instead, I would like to usher you into a seat which I believe, as a fan and as an academic, reveals just how closely India and its films have woven their dreams and hopes into each other in less than one century, and how much our films reflect not only the social history of our times, but also our negotiations and struggles with broader dilemmas as human beings. I do not claim unquestionable authority as either a fan or a scholar on this subject—there are more passionate fans and more erudite scholars around, for sure—but I do stand by the one belief that I had put forth in writing some years ago. A few days after the tragic events in America on 11 September 2001, I wrote a short essay saying that, in an age when Hollywood (and Washington) seemed to be all about 'saving the world' by destroying it, Indian cinema could be a great global cultural resource for imagining ways of living and relating that would be necessary to actually save the world. While I do not mean to make our films seem any more messianic than they may be, I do hope to make an argument that some of the ideals celebrated in Indian cinema have kept alive certain ways of looking at the world and understanding ourselves that students of India and the media need to take seriously.

Indian Cinema in the Classroom

My belief that we have much to learn from Indian cinema and what it means to its audiences comes as much from professional predilections as from personal experience. As someone who teaches media studies for a living, I have the opportunity not only to examine cinema as a fan or a critic, but also to pay attention to how some bigger issues that concern the world may be illumined through what we see in our media. I approach Indian cinema in this book primarily as a story about how one part of the world has been dealing with what is essentially a global experience—that of modernity. It is a story about our coming to terms with the way the world and our lives have come to be shaped in the most recent five hundred years of history, in the wake, as it were, of what Ashis Nandy (2001) calls 'Europe's age of arrogance in the tropics' (p. 7). It is a story that speaks to our pleasures and our struggles with the transformations in life that have taken place on a magnitude that was unprecedented in history. In the past five hundred years, the whole world has been transformed through colonization and its aftermath. People around the world are now left with new conditions to live in—cities instead of villages, anonymous communities of strangers instead of extended families, frozen foods (or famine for the other half) instead of local produce, bio-bureaucrats instead of healers, and, most of all, strange new mass-mediated ideas about one's own self and one's place in the world. That, in a few lines, is the big picture against which what cinema means to India is best understood. Indian cinema is a story not about just modernity, but postcolonial modernity.

From their earliest years, the films of India have served not merely as entertainment or an escape, but also as a source of idealism for audiences in their encounter with postcolonial modernity. In some ways, our films have welcomed the modern, celebrating the breakdown of old feudal barriers to communal mobility. In other ways, they have resisted it, if nothing else, at least by positing family ties and values like sacrifice over modern notions of individualism and self-interest. They have been about what it means to be Indian, a concern all too important in a nation with too many cultural differences to ever be complacent about being one, and they have also been very simply about what it means to be human. They have been as much about political issues like nationalism, as they have been about philosophical issues, like life. In the ideals of our cinema, we see traces of some of the great men who made India, men like Gandhi and Nehru, and echoes of their own negotiations of modernity. We can also see the responses cinema has made to the crises and travails of our times, whether it is the failure of the government or the rise of terrorism. Finally, as we enter into an increasingly global context for Indian cinema and its study, it is important to recognize that it continues to maintain a strong engagement with questions that have vanished from the purview of cultural expression in other countries. As Rachel Dwyer (2006) writes:

> Many of the arts in the West no longer pay attention to minds and souls, virtues, love, duty, self-sacrifice, and character, but instead concentrate on bodies, from surfaces to orifices. Hindi films still ask important questions about bodies, souls, morals and selves (p. 167).

I think that the broader questions that arise when we look at Indian cinema seriously are of universal relevance. In the classes that I have taught about India and Indian cinema in the United States, what we have learnt is not only about what makes India or Indian cinema 'different', but also what makes its insights into what it means to be a human being in the world today far more relevant than its frequent frivolities would suggest. Indian cinema is not just about India, but about deeper questions that transcend borders of language, race, and taste. For example, watching the film *Mission Kashmir* in my 'Media, Stereotyping and Violence' class in the aftermath of 9/11/2001 led to questions that I think America and the world needed to ask at that time. Is violence really crucial to religion, or is it politics that makes it that way? How do we distinguish justice from revenge? Is human nature inherently violent? Are we really witnessing a 'clash of civilizations'? And of course, on a somewhat less serious note, why on earth would a genocidal militant stop to dance to a bumblebee song? Fortunately for us, questions like the last one are perhaps the hardest to answer. The rest, once we enter the theatre, are sorted out with little room for ethical or narrative ambiguity. Indian cinema really knows exactly the right thing to say to the most profound questions facing humanity. We just need to listen the right way.

The Bollywood Nation

Although the book discusses Indian cinema more or less chronologically, starting with the mythological films of the early twentieth century and ending with a number of recent, post-globalization genres, it does not aim to provide an extensive history of cinema. Instead, my goal is to explore a number of important themes that have not only characterized the films in each of these periods, but have sometimes been the defining concerns of India in these periods as well. Sometimes, these themes overlap with genres, and sometimes, they span different genres altogether. I focus on these themes rather than on genres strictly because they enable us to address not only the films, but the contexts of these films a little more seriously as well. In later sections, I also address television, not only for the closeness with which its programming has followed cinema, but also because it has been of great importance in the last two decades.

I should also add that while I refer to numerous academic studies of Indian cinema, I do not necessarily ground this book in any one theory of cinema as such. Some scholars of Indian cinema have proposed that we should examine it

fundamentally through the lens of various approaches like
Marxism, psychoanalysis, feminism, and film theory. But the
perspective that I privilege in this book is really that of the
films themselves. For example, the opening scene in *Raja
Harischandra*, the first film made in India, shows what to
most viewers would seem like the queen fussing over the
prince, but to more scholarly observers as something else.
My interest in this book, in other words, is mainly in the
stories in the films and how they have been told. At the same
time, I do attempt to situate some of these meanings in the
context of broader questions about India's experiences of
postcolonial modernity.

I am aware of the pros and cons of such an approach, but I
hope that way I can suitably address this book to both
academic and non-academic readers. There is a chance that
serious students of cinema will find not enough film theory;
and non-academic readers will find my arguments too serious
for a book, after all, about cinema. There is another limitation
I should mention in terms of the choice of films for this book.
I focus on popular cinema, and do not engage with the rich
world of art or parallel cinema. While my focus is mainly on
Hindi cinema, I do engage on occasion with Telugu cinema
as well, not only out of native familiarity but also because of
its relevance to discussions of some genres, like the
mythological.

The chapters in this book are organized around four broad
topics which suggest either an important predilection for
Indians in general, or for a particular period in our history.
These are: God, Country, Home and World. These
correspond, approximately, to a sequence of moments in
recent history. In the chapter titled 'God', I look at what is

considered to be the 'founding genre' of Indian cinema—the mythological. Focusing mainly on films from the earlier part of the twentieth century, I discuss what they tell us about popular Indian views of God in general. In the next chapter, 'Country', I discuss the cinema of the post-Independence period as an example of how we began to think of ourselves as Indians. I situate the films of Raj Kapoor in the context of Nehru's India, and those of Amitabh Bachchan in terms of the political disenchantment that had set in by the 1970s. In this chapter, I also address a question often asked of popular Indian cinema—Why are our films not enamoured by the notion of realism? In the third chapter, 'Home', I move away from Hindi cinema to address a range of developments that took place in the 1980s, including the rise of television, the mythological serials *Ramayan* and *Mahabharat*, and the fascinating journey of the great Telugu actor N.T. Rama Rao (NTR) into politics. I situate these developments in the context of the changes that began to take place in our social and economic priorities during that time. In the final chapter, 'World', I look at the vast changes in media and culture since globalization and consider a number of themes in recent cinema, including the rise of the yuppie hero and the diasporic desi. I conclude with a discussion about the question of violence in terrorist and gangster films, and the ideal that came to be known as 'Gandhigiri'. Finally, in an epilogue titled 'Life', I propose some ways of thinking about how the ideals in our films have represented our emotional and ethical negotiations with the conditions of modernity, and what I believe the core principle underlying these ideals has been.

1

GOD

Raja Harischandra
Draupadi Vastrapaharanam
Sant Tukaram
Tyagayya
Bhukailasa
Maya Bazaar
Sri Krishna Tulabharam

GOD MAY WELL BE THE SINGLE BIGGEST CONCERN OF INDIAN CINEMA, directly or indirectly. The first films made in India were 'mythologicals'. After Independence, as 'social' films became more prolific in Hindi, some of the greatest and most popular films associated with what some would call the Golden Age of Telugu and Tamil cinema were still about the gods. It would seem that each new mass medium in India, following its emergence, has to pass through a phase of paying tribute to the stories of the gods. In the 1980s, when India witnessed a massive growth in television, the biggest stories on the new medium were once again *Ramayan* and *Mahabharat*. In more recent years, the rise of animation has once again led to a mythological revival of sort, with new films, TV series, and DVDs being made on Hanuman, Ganesha and, of course, the ever popular Krishna. If we look beyond the audiovisual media, we can see that even in the popular print medium of the comic book, the stories of the gods as they appeared in the *Amar Chitra Katha* series have been unsurpassed by any other comics series. Given the rapidity with which new communication technologies have spread in India since the 1990s, it may not be surprising to find the stories of the gods emerging in ever newer forms, and a mythological for mobile phones may well be the next communications avatar in which we will watch them.

Despite the temptation, especially in some academic and journalistic circles, to view this phenomenon as nothing more than an echo of Cecil B. De Mille's quip that 'God is box office', the fact is that we cannot begin to understand how India understands itself without some acknowledgement of what God means in a popular sense—which means in a *cinematic* sense—to a large extent as well. When Phalke's silent films about Krishna and Hanuman began to be watched in the early twentieth century, what was going through viewers' minds was not just 'entertainment' in the way we see it now, but something more astounding, unsurpassed in their experience. Chidananda Das Gupta (1989) describes such a moment evocatively:

> As the screen lit up in the vast night in the open . . . a primeval dream unfolded before the eyes in which the gods lived . . . for the devout Hindu, it was almost like the traditional glimpse of God in a dream. (p. 13)

Cinema elevated Krishna, Rama, Hanuman, the gods, their companions and great devotees, who had abided in the popular imagination for centuries, to a new level of spectacle, theatricality and magic. Das Gupta adds:

> Previously, the country of the gods had existed only in the mind's eye . . . now, suddenly, these imagined scenes were there on the screen, as reality. (p. 12)

It is this sense of reality that I try to explore, to some extent, in this chapter. India has not only made more films about the divine than perhaps any other country (and, within India, perhaps that honour falls even more specifically upon Telugu cinema), but what is unique about them is that these films were made not by religious organizations as propaganda, but by generations of film-makers who ranged from nationalists, devotees and social reformers to savvy media entrepreneurs. What is also interesting is that in all the hundreds of titles made about the lives of the gods and goddesses, there have been few controversies along the lines of *The Da Vinci Code* or the Danish cartoons. However, scholarship about religion in Indian cinema is yet to arrive at a suitable appreciation of these finer points. As Dwyer (2006)—whose own work has been a welcome exception—writes, there has in general been too little research done on religion in Indian cinema. What little has been done has largely failed to emphasize the distinctions between what religion, in the media or elsewhere, means to its believers, and what its political implications have been. As she points out, most discussions about religion and Indian cinema tend to focus not on the meaning of religion but on political questions about how religious communities and ideologies are represented.

The question of how the divine is interpreted in a popular sense by media audiences has been rarely addressed. For example, reading some of the scholarship on religion in Indian media, one might get the impression that the only thing that happens when Indians consume such media is that they become religious extremists! At the risk of using academic jargon too early in this book, I would like to invoke one concept from audience research literature to explain this phenomenon—we have had many critical readings of Hindu texts in the academy, but the academy has largely failed to even talk about what the 'preferred reading' of these texts would be. Particularly in the Western context, where there has been a history since colonial times of misrepresentation of India in general and Hinduism in particular, the present

trend in academics has failed to understand some realities
about how Indians understand God, and how their films
have played their own role in it.

Since the days of Phalke's films, and even before, the stories
of the gods have had many significant meanings for people in
India which we are only beginning to hear about. The
mythological stage plays of the theatre groups of India during
colonial times, like those of the Parsi Theatre and the Surabhi
group, were retelling the 'myths' to bring out ethical messages
as were appropriate for the times (Hansen, 2006).
Mythological films during the 1920s and 1930s were seen as
an allegory for the freedom movement, and one film in
particular—*Bhakta Vidur* (1921)—was even the subject of
much British consternation for its lead character's supposed
resemblance to Mahatma Gandhi. The saint films of the
1930s and 1940s, like the Marathi *Sant Tukaram* (1936) and
the Telugu *Tyagayya* (1946), advocated the virtues of
egalitarianism and devotion. After Independence, it was in
the stories of the gods that some of the greatest stars of South
Indian cinema came to be accorded their near-divine status
by fans. Yet, often, the only thing we hear about as having
come out of this rich media phenomenon is the much more
recent political fall-out of Hindu nationalism. I disagree, and
instead propose a different way of approaching mythological
cinema in this chapter.

My emphasis here is not so much on either the social
history of the mythological cinema as a form, nor on the
politics of its caste and gender implications, since other
scholarship seems to have adequately addressed such
concerns. I would like to shift the emphasis to the stories of
the gods themselves, and also to the deeper beliefs that inform
our relationship to these stories. In order to do this, I propose

that we turn away from the identity-political implications of mythological media, towards what I think is the all-important semiotic fulcrum of mythology—the morals of the stories, the ideals, as it were. It is out of deference to such concerns that I have titled this chapter not 'Religion', but 'God'. I explore the broad question of how God is ideally understood in mythological cinema using four main themes—'God as One (and Many)', 'God as One of Us', 'God as Good', and 'God, Devotion, Real Life'. I cover mythological, devotional and religious cinema in general over a fairly wide period, and also step beyond the films themselves in some parts to the stories in general, since they have been repeated in numerous films. I assume familiarity with the stories here, and will of course issue the disclaimer that I am indeed aware of the existence of other subversive renderings of the epics. I just don't know them all that well, and would rather stick to the versions that we all know, since popular films do that too. I also do not reduce the meanings of mythology to their historical contexts, as if Krishna meant one thing in the Nehruvian era and an altogether different thing once the Hindutva movement got started. At the same time, I do touch on the religious thought of one key figure, Mahatma Gandhi, in the last section of this chapter. This is because the question of what the mythological means, especially to a people struggling with conditions of postcolonial modernity, is closely related to how its greatest critic also understood religion.

God as One (and Many)

If there is one basic—if not always explicitly expressed—theme in mythological cinema and popular understandings of religion, it is that there is one God. To an unfamiliar observer, this may seem like an odd claim to make, since the proliferation of multiple gods in Hinduism, and in films and TV serials about them in more recent times, would suggest the opposite. It is not uncommon, particularly in popular Western publications, to hear the claim that Hinduism has three hundred and thirty million gods (a point to which I return below). It has also become quite common to hear, in the writings of concerned South Asian intellectuals and activists, that Hindu 'fundamentalists' are seeking to reinvent Hinduism as a monotheistic religion along Judaeo-Christian lines. The multiplicity of gods in Hinduism is indeed a fact, but it has of late become a way of making different sorts of points. We could celebrate it as a sign of Hinduism's plurality, diversity and ability to accommodate the existence of different faiths. But there are also those who fear that the label of polytheism is sometimes used by latter-day orientalists and non-Hindu fundamentalists to denigrate Hinduism and misrepresent it as a 'pagan' religion, so superstitious that it needs a god for everything.

Indian cinema may not have strayed into the finer points of these intellectual arguments, but it has—explicitly or otherwise—stayed true to a deeper sensibility in Hindu philosophy about the question of one God or many gods. It may be safe to say that the scores of films that have been made about Krishna, Rama, Shiva, Ganesha, Hanuman, the goddesses, saints and, of course, sacred serpents do not ever take a fundamentally monotheistic view (e.g., advocating that Krishna or Rama is God and no one else), nor do they represent what some modern observers call polytheism (depicting each of the gods as separate and equal). Instead, the view of the divine in Indian cinema may be described, a propos Hindu sensibilities in general, as one which sees God both as One and Many. The multiplicity of deities does not contradict the belief in One God, and the contradiction is one which arises largely as a result of (mis)perception, out of the limitations of modern, literal ways of thinking. The much quoted figure of three hundred and thirty million gods is, as mythologist Devdutt Pattanaik (2006) writes, 'a metaphor for the countless forms by which the divine makes itself accessible to the human mind' (p. 5).

The idea of 'form' is central to the way the divine is conceived in Hindu philosophy (and is an important consideration in mythological cinema as well, as I show in a later section in this chapter). As Arvind Sharma (2000) points out, Hinduism does believe in the idea of one ultimate reality, Brahman, which is comparable, according to him, to 'Yahweh . . . in Judaism; God in Christianity; Allah in Islam; Nirvana in Theravada Buddhism; the Buddha in Mahayana Buddhism; Heaven in Confucianism and Tao in Taoism' (p. 1). However, the one ultimate reality—God, so to speak—is thought of in two ways: as having no form or attribute (guna) on the one hand; and as possessing certain forms, even personalities, on the other. When we speak of God in a Hindu sense, we are therefore not in any way contradicting ourselves when we also speak of *gods*, like Shiva or Vishnu. Although, as Sharma points out, different schools of thought in Hinduism have accorded different values to the relationship between formless and personified God, no school denies the existence of both. In this sense, it may be possible to speak of Hinduism, as Sharma suggests as being polytheistic, henotheistic, and monotheistic.

The view of God as one and many was not necessarily an explicit predilection in early mythological cinema (it arises frequently in later 'socials', especially with a view to advocating Hindu–Muslim unity), but certainly underlies the ethical lessons underlying numerous episodes. The most common narrative device in the mythologicals, through which this point is made, often has to do with the misrecognition of a divinity by another character. Sometimes, this misrecognition is merely a question of misplaced faith, and whole tales are drawn out to make the point that even great devotees can err if they become fixed upon one particular form of God over another. In various films, we find episodes in which even those closest to the gods are humbled—Hanuman, Arjuna, Jambavanth, all find themselves in fights over Rama or Krishna, only to learn they are all one. Sometimes, the scope and consequences of this error are extreme to the point of villainy. Ravana, as we see in the 1940 film *Bhukailasa*, is an ardent devotee of Lord Shiva. But, in his foolish arrogance, he also remains an implacable foe of Lord Vishnu. His devotion to one form of God ultimately fails him, because he cannot see the underlying unity of all forms of God, and his actions (precipitated in no small measure by the ever-conspiratorial Narada) spell his own doom.

Recognizing the unity underlying the different forms of God may have been an important sensibility only occasionally referenced explicitly in the early mythologicals, but it was presented as an almost paramount imperative in another early gènre of Indian cinema: the devotional or 'saint film', as Dwyer calls it. Some of the most outstanding films of the 1930s and '40s—the decades which are, perhaps not just coincidentally, also coterminous with the height of Gandhian nationalism—were about the great saints of the Bhakti or devotional tradition. Films like *Sant Tukaram* and *Tyagayya* extolled the virtues of simple devotion over hollow ritual and the attendant politics of status and hierarchy that went with it. In *Tyagayya*, a well-known episode from the composer-saint's life is developed into an intense emotional and spiritual quest. Exasperated by his younger brother's refusal to sing at the royal court, Tyagayya's older brother steals his sacred idols from his shrine and throws them into the river. Grief-struck, Tyagayya—portrayed by the great elder of early Telugu cinema Chittooru Nagaiah—wanders through the country in search of his gods. Finally, after visiting numerous holy temples, he has a dream. All the deities he has seen so far appear one after another, and tell him what was missing in his quest. 'Silly fellow,' God says to Tyagayya, 'how long are you going to suffer this anguish about your lost idols and search everywhere without getting to know Me, the omnipresent? *Wake up!*' Once Tyagayya realizes the folly of form, he finds his purloined deities (who miraculously rise from the riverbed of the Kaveri) and attains the degree of sainthood he was always meant to.

The realization of God as one, as formless, as truth (a central idea in Gandhian thought too, as I discuss later), may have been presented as the ultimate goal in the narrative of the saint film, but Hindu mythology and mythological cinema are in general more engaged with God in his various forms. It is in the stories and the films about Krishna and Rama, for example, that we see a lot more of the popular religious sensibility playing out. In the following section, I examine some of the reasons for this phenomenon. The ultimate philosophical goal, the paramount ideal as it were, may have been the realization of God, but in getting there, in getting through the ups and downs of everyday human life as it were, it is always the gods, and their ever familiar stories, that the films and their audiences have turned to.

God as One of Us

The image of Lord Vishnu reclining on the coils of Adi-Sesha, the eternal serpent afloat on a vast sea of milk, a dazzling array of cosmic phenomena like stars and galaxies spinning above, may seem an unlikely example to depict the notion of God as 'one of us'. Great blue-skinned gods, with further gods meditating in the lotus flower rising from their navels, watched over by the thousand heads of a celestial serpent may seem quite reminiscent of the outlandish 'thousand-armed' gods and goddesses that the Western imagination sometimes confronts when it pictures Hinduism. But in many mythological films, the primordial Lord Vishnu in majestic repose is the scene with which a more down-to-earth story begins, and this is often the story in which the gods are not merely up there in the sky, but are here, in human form, caught up in the nitty-gritty of every detail of human life from family bonds to political struggles.

But, before the great God becomes one of us, there is usually a problem for which His help must be sought. A typical opening scene in a mythological film might begin with an overview of a demon king gone wild on power (and interestingly, these demon kings earn their powers through great austerities and then worship themselves, making the point useful to all those who worry about the pieties of the selfish—that seeking God's favour for bad reasons is ultimately a bad choice). His minions rampage across the earth and the heavens, driving out the demigods who preside over the natural elements, chasing the venerable rishis and their noble wives from their hermitages, desecrating their sacred fires. They harm the good villagers too, taxing them, taking away their produce, burning their villages. Finally, Bhu Devi— Mother Earth—makes a weary sign or two that she cannot sustain such depredations any more. At this time, the rishis, the demigods, and sometimes even the ordinary people rush to the gates of Vishnu's abode. They beseech him with extended arms, and with songs and verses. Finally, still smiling serenely, Vishnu grants them the boon they seek. He will appear among them, in human form, as an avatar, and deliver them from their woes. He may even choose to explain at this time the exact complex of curses and karmic burdens and prophecies that have led to this moment, and add the assurance that Mother Lakshmi will also incarnate along with him, to be his wife in his earthly avatar.

Thus begin the tales of the gods in their avatars, in their all-too-human forms. The mythologicals, whether the earliest silent films or the later classics from the Golden Age of Telugu cinema, are as much about human stories as they are about a divinity. I do not say this to imply in the Western sense that the mythologicals are nothing more than myths in the same order as, say, fairy tales. Instead, it is in the recollection of the actions of the gods in human form and human situations that certain deeper philosophical sensibilities are often understood. Mullapudi Ramana (2006), the writer half of the legendary Telugu director–writer duo Bapu–Ramana, sees mythology essentially as the democratization of philosophy. According to Ramana, Vyasa wrote the epics because ideas about divinity had previously been too esoteric and inaccessible to ordinary people. He says that the myths are ultimately about teaching ethical living, regardless of how one chooses to believe in them.

The way that mythology expresses such a democratic, popular sense of ethical conduct is by situating the gods firmly into the relational dimension of human existence; into what is our all-too-human lot as sons, brothers, fathers, friends and such. It is in these relationships—particularly in the stories from the epics—that we see the more philosophical concerns like duty, fate, truth and freedom play out. Even loftier concerns like cosmology are ultimately made meaningful through the question of how we engage with one another as human beings, in our daily living. Thus, the central predilection of the Mahabharata, according to Chaturvedi Badrinath (2006) is very simply, the relationship between the self and the other. As the self and the other are inseparable, the Mahabharata seems to say, it is only by getting our relationship with the other right that we get our relationship with our own selves right (and the other way around as well). And the situations that the Mahabharata explores as the contexts for these strivings, Badrinath says, are not on some mystical plane involving the 'big Self' but simply in the mundane situations of daily life.

Such a sensibility is central to some of the most popular mythological films from what viewers often describe as the golden age of Telugu cinema. Unlike some of the later versions of the epic films, some of the most popular mythological films focus not on a pedagogic panorama of well-known episodes, but instead on minor, seemingly unimportant tales. *Maya Bazar* (1956), a legendary film in which NTR plays Krishna, passes over the more well-known events from the

Mahabharata, such as the game of dice and the exile, and instead focuses on a charming, humorous tale that generations of audiences find endearing. The main conflict in this story is romantic. Krishna's niece Sasirekha (played by Savitri) is in love with Arjuna's son, Abhimanyu (portrayed by Akkineni Nageswara Rao). But her father, the bold but easily fooled Balarama (Gummadi), has been smooth-talked into fixing her marriage with the son of Duryodhana, the villainous Kaurava prince. Krishna proves the diplomatic puppetmaster in this story, but one more memorable character appears to help him play the game—Ghatotkacha, the half-demon son of Bheema. With his magical powers and boisterous humour, Ghatotkacha takes the Kauravas for a ride, and helps the young lovers unite as well. *Maya Bazar*'s appeal is of course as much in its story as in its stars. It is indelibly associated with the greats of Telugu cinema—NTR plays a graceful, all-knowing and just-so clever Krishna in this film, and S.V. Ranga Rao's mighty and majestic Ghatotkacha leaves children laughing to this day. But the performance and the beautiful songs and sets aside, the film also reveals an interesting feature of the Telugu mythological in its Golden Age—it is a story about something not very important from a doctrinal view of religion at all.

Some of the most popular mythologicals of this time, in fact, deal precisely with the utter triviality of Krishna's daily life. In *Shri Krishna Tulabharam* (1966), for example, we see an unusual predicament involving Krishna's consorts brought about by instigations of the omnipresent Narada. In *Shri Krishnarjuna Yuddham* (1962), we see Krishna and Arjuna brought into conflict over the matter of a curse and a boon, and, of course, sorting everything out. In these films, we do

not see Krishna in his most famous religious role delivering
the message of the Gita on the battlefield to Arjuna. We see
Krishna the brother-in-law, uncle, husband and friend. It is
in these everyday roles that we may appreciate the
philosophical imperatives of mythology too. The
'mythologicals' are thus less about the whims and fancies of
the gods, and more about what happens when they are
enmeshed in the web of human relationships, in the quotidian
heart of the human condition, as it were. They are, hence, as
much about the gods as they are about the people around
them, who range from avatars of other gods or demigods,
wise men and women, to just ordinary people. Some of the
stories, like the *Maya Bazar*, are on the whole happy, and
suggest that a sense of playfulness doesn't necessarily go
against the order of things in our lives. But when we get down
to the more serious aspects of the stories of the lives of the
gods, we see the dilemmas and challenges; the limits of our
own selves as humans that remind us why we need God in
the first place. As Badrinath (2006) writes:

> [I]n every act of relating, it is given to man to transcend
> history—not as any ethical 'ought', but as a spiritual necessity,
> indeed as an emotional necessity of living. People achieve it
> all the time; they go beyond given contexts and their histories.
> And that is how the sanity of human living is possible. And
> that is how friendship and love are still possible. (p. 21)

Even if God, in his cosmic forms as Vishnu or Shiva, seems
bigger than history (although not above the occasional rishi's
curse), the constraints that the favourite avatars face are all
essentially human ones. As one of us, God is never too
removed from 'history'. Rama falls from the high affection of

his stepmother Kaikeyi for no reason other than her conspiracy with a disgruntled maid. He goes into exile, leaving behind his grieving father, distraught brothers, loyal subjects and, of course, the throne. In his little hermitage, his idyll is once again shattered when Sita is abducted. He searches for her like a madman. He does battle, many times. Even after he returns, he is bound by his sense of duty to send away his beloved wife. He loses her, again, and again. Krishna, too, grows up into a world wrecked by intrigue and war. His childhood in Gokula is a pastoral paradise, a paragon for the world of innocent children, notwithstanding the occasional disturbance from a demon assassin who proves no match for him anyway. Yet, he too has to go, leaving his aching stepmother Yasodha and the young boys and girls of his village. He goes in and out of a web of conspiracies and cruelties as he steers his cousins, the Pandavas, to a return from their own exile, and through the great war. He finds himself the victim of slander and false accusation in the matter of the Syamantaka gem, and fights formidable opponents to clear his name. Unlike most other avatars, Krishna's passing finds a mention, even if briefly in the stories. He is killed by a hunter who mistakes his foot for the head of a deer. Beloved Krishna!

Terms like duty and virtue, which are often used in association with religious stories, miss the immediacy of the human conditions in which the gods are known to their devotees. Their lives are not unlike those of the people who have heard their stories. There are accusations, recriminations, exiles, lost kingdoms, lost loves, wars, hatreds, jealousies. There are all the things life in the world is about. But there are the reminders, that 'friendship and love are still possible', that there is an order, perhaps one of causality, one of destiny and equally one of agency, to which striving may be directed, not in isolation, but in relationships, in families, in societies, in the matter of living as a whole. That is the assurance we have from knowing that God is one of us too, and that, in some ways, is the most exalted of ideals mythological cinema presents to its audiences.

God as Good

The familiarity that we accord God in the mythologicals does not however mean that he's entirely like one of us. There are two aspects to the ways in which mythology and, to a large extent popular mythological cinema too, accords an unfailingly positive characterization to God and his avatars— the aesthetic, and the ethical. There are conventions, in other words, in terms of how a film would depict a god, not only in terms of appearance, but also his actions. Since popular contemporary Hinduism, like any tradition, is one that has been constantly reimagined, these conventions are by no means set in stone. As M.S. Reddy (2006), a producer of Telugu mythological films and translator of the Ramayana, says, no one really knows what the gods looked like. It was left to the imagination of successive artists and devotees. However, even in the absence of strict scriptural conventions about, say, what sort of clothes or ornaments Krishna or Rama would wear, we find that there have indeed been certain norms in mythological films. Some of these have changed even as media culture has changed, but it is useful to consider the philosophical imperatives behind the 'forms' in which the gods are depicted.

The mythologicals have leaned towards pomp and grandeur

from their early days. As Dwyer (2006) writes, the oldest surviving talkie in India, *Ayodhya Ka Raja* (1932), features 'spectacles of processions of elephants, dances, an ornate palace and court' (p. 31). By the time the star system began to dominate cinema in the next decades, it was only natural that the greatest of stars came to portray the greatest of gods, at least in the case of South Indian cinema. The emphasis on grand personas, rich costumes and ornaments, and a duly majestic palatial setting whenever appropriate, are all an indelible part of the mythological aesthetic tradition. The stark austerity of alternative visions such as Peter Brook's intense stage adaptation of the Mahabharata is often not the preferred form in which the tales of gods are expected by Indian audiences. The emphasis on costumes and decorativeness—especially in some of the more recent televised versions—sometimes also lends itself to criticism of resemblance to kitsch; but, at least in principle, the question of adornment in mythological cinema is related to deeper concerns about the ideal of beauty and its sacred implications.

The ideal of beauty is important to the representation of the divine in Hindu philosophy. As the phrase 'Satyam Shivam Sundaram' (Truth, Auspiciousness and Beauty) implies, what is believed to be true is also considered to be beautiful (K. Singh, 2003). One reason Indian arts in general value the notion of beauty in communicating the divine is that experience of the sacred is generally understood in Indian thought to be closely linked to emotional experience (as I show in the next section). The sacred is understood not merely through rational discourse, but through immersion in emotional states or rasas. From the rasa perspective, beauty may be seen, as Makarand Paranjape (2003) suggests, as the

combination of two rasas, shringar and adbhuta—
sensuousness and wonder. Paranjape further adds that
soundarya ('beauty-ness') is related to all the major rasas,
through presence or absence. In the mythological films, we
can see soundarya being an important concern, and expressed
in various forms. As Harsha Dehejia (2003) writes, the ideal
of beauty is invoked in art not only through 'adornment'
(costume, make-up, gesture, sets, in the case of cinema) but
also through narrative (plot, action, dialogues).

Although some of the mythological films of the early
twentieth century, such as *Sampoorna Ramayanam* (1936),
seem like nothing more than filmed versions of the stage
presentations popular in those times, we also find films from
the same era like *Draupadi Vastrapaharanam* that feature
elephants, chariots, palaces and well-known singer-actors in
important roles. Being able to sing and act was an important
requisite for films of that period, given the rich musical and
poetic dimension of dialogues. As the revered character actor
Gummadi (2006) says, one of the reasons the mythological
genre declined in the Telugu film industry in the later decades
was simply because there were few actors who could do
justice to what he calls 'bhasha soundaryam' (linguistic
beauty).

The rise of the great stars also coincided with the aesthetic
sensibilities of the mythological genre, especially in the 1950s
and '60s. Reddy (2006) attributes the prominence and
eventual decline of mythology in the Telugu film industry to
the particular set of actors who came together at that time.
Telugu viewers, he says, have come to associate certain stars
so closely with their divine roles that it has been difficult to
find, with their passing or retirement, new actors with the

same degree of perceived affinity. This, he says, is one of the reasons he made a mythological film a few years ago cast entirely with children—the beautifully staged *Bala Ramayanam* (1997). After having become accustomed to associating Krishna with NTR, Satyabhama with Jamuna, Narada with Kanta Rao and Ghatotkacha with S.V. Ranga Rao, Telugu viewers expect a grandeur for mythological roles for which it is not easy to find suitable 'paatradharis', as Reddy says.

One reason for the exalted status film actors found through mythological roles is described by Das Gupta (1989). He observes that traditional stage actors, especially in village plays, lost the charisma they acquired on the stage in divine roles when they returned to their quotidian realities the morning after. Film actors, on the other hand, became known to their audiences largely through their on-screen image and, even when they met fans in person, they sometimes did so in the mythological costume, as if Lord Krishna himself was giving darshan. At the same time, there is no doubt that the sort of acting that was brought into cinema had its roots in the stage traditions. Das Gupta writes:

> Naturalism in acting and staging were hardly possible; the voice had to be raised in order to be heard, the gesture had to be grand in order to be seen.

Although in later years, and especially in its new avatars of television and animation, the mythological genre moved far from its traditional conventions derived from the stage, aesthetic expectations did remain important for some. As Dwyer observes, unlike the star status that mythological cinema acquired in South India, it became a B-grade genre in

Hindi, with the only redemption perhaps being the occasionally uplifting overlap with the 'pehlwan' or strongman film featuring Dara Singh. In the more recent set of televised mythological serials which have been dubbed and telecast across a range of languages and channels in India, it is more common to find aesthetic issues when they arise because of regional differences. A common complaint I have heard about how the divine messenger Narada is depicted in some of the Hindi mythologicals has to do with the insinuation that he is a jester of sorts, sporting a tuft of hair with a flower atop. Even in terms of costumes, ornaments and sets, there are differences in aesthetic preferences in various regional productions. To some extent, these differences may be simply because of the much greater investment made in the mythological genre in Telugu and Tamil in comparison to Hindi. When the acclaimed artist and director Bapu turned to TV a few years ago, his signature artistic vision was very much in evidence in his production of the Bhagavatham for Eenadu Television.

The formal history of how the gods have been depicted in cinema has been a negotiation between non-modern ideals and modern developments in communications technology, art, and social context. In recent years, there has also been a tendency towards a new aesthetic which we could call 'God as Tough'. In recent calendar art, for example, we find the gods looking more muscular. Even the great South Indian saint Raghavendra Swamy, who was often portrayed with a modest round belly, appears in some recent images in a trim body and with a trimmer beard. Some of these changes, particularly the proliferation of more muscular images of Rama, have, of course, led to legitimate concerns about the growing influence of Hindu nationalist sensibilities on religious depictions as well. There has, at the same time, been an opposite tendency too. With the easy traffic in images since globalization and the advent of computers and the Internet, there has been a tendency to misuse sacred images and symbols. The gods have been depicted in numerous inappropriate forms and contexts, in India and especially abroad. My view is that some things are indeed sacred, and there is something to be learnt from respecting the integrity of the forms in which the divine has been represented. As Telugu cinema's favourite Narada, actor Kanta Rao (2006), says, despite being occasionally ridiculed, every part of Ganesha's 'aakaram' (form) has a lesson for us. Ganesha's small eyes, according to him, imply that we should see the world with humility. If an elephant god could do that, I am sure some of those who take artistic liberties with him could too.

The second aspect of the ideal of God as good pertains to the ethical positions that mythologicals take with regard to the actions of their divine characters. There are numerous questions one could ask about some of the actions of the avatars in the stories which do not seem ethical. Some avatars, such as Krishna, are sometimes perceived as being less than straightforward in their dealings, resorting to trickery and favouritism. There are also questions that one may ask about some actions, particularly, as they pertain to women; such as Rama's abandonment of Sita on the strength of a washerman's whisper. Such questions are seldom expressed in the mythologicals as a way to criticize the gods, but instead are often depicted in the narrative as choices made out of larger ethical considerations. For example, Rama's decision to send Sita away is depicted in the film *Lava Kusa* (1963) as an agonizing one for him; he does it not because he really doubts her virtue, but instead as a sacrifice of his own attachments for the sake of his duties as a king. In a memorable scene in *Maya Bazar*, a magical box, which shows images of the favourite person of whoever looks into it, reveals that Krishna is fond of the villainous uncle Shakuni. This revelation startles onlookers, but Krishna insists that he has his reasons and no one should be puzzled by it. The reason, we may infer, is that Shakuni will ultimately set in motion the events that will lead to the destruction of the villainous Kauravas.

An even more important question that arises on this note pertains to how God may be idealized as good when his avatars seem to carry weapons and commit numerous acts of violence. Although such questions may have become more common in recent years with the rise of militant Hindu nationalism, and were perhaps less relevant in the earlier heyday of mythological cinema, it is useful to address them and make a distinction between the political (ab)uses of myth and their more mainstream cultural and spiritual implications. Like any tradition, popular Hinduism has been open to interpretation from different sources and with different interests in mind. The Bhagavad Gita, for example, seems an inevitable example for such criticisms in particular. Krishna's sermon to Arjuna takes place on the eve of imminent battle. Arjuna hesitates, as any decent person would; and it is Krishna who talks him into taking up his arms again. It is easy to misconstrue the Gita as a call for violence, or, as some observers have said, as a call for one to do his 'caste duty'. The Gita has been interpreted by numerous other commentators who have seen much in it beyond a mere call for caste-duty or violence. For an apostle of non-violence like

Mahatma Gandhi, the message of the Gita was resonant with ahimsa, rather than any mere call to violent action.

The slaying of villains and demons by the gods is more appropriately understood in the context of the narrative and the philosophy. Even if Rama and Krishna seem to incarnate in human form for the sole purpose of slaying a demon, their actions are not marked by rage, hatred or a lack of patience. As someone whose vision has informed so many Telugu mythological films, Ramana's (2006) views best express this sensibility. He says, 'God's work is never killing.' Instead, God's main tasks in his avatars are to propagate 'samskaraam' (culture or decency) and not 'samharaam' (slaying). Finally, for good measure, Ramana also adds, 'God always gives a long rope.' In this sense, evident in the one hundred times Krishna forgives Sisupala, violence is never the first option.

Although there have been numerous transformations over time in the aesthetics of violence in mythological cinema and television, at least in principle the ethics of when and how gods turns to violence is an important consideration in the popular sensibility. Suffice it to note that no matter how many flying arrows, whirling discuses and decapitated heads we see in a mythological film, the notion of jealous and warring gods who mutilate their own fathers as we find in Greek mythology is completely out of place in popular Indian mythology and cinema. Even if there is deception and violence in their actions, the gods must also follow certain codes of right and wrong. They may perform violent actions when necessary, but they cannot be cruel by nature, or capricious, unjust or selfish. Their kindness must extend beyond their own near ones to all humans and to all creatures. The goodness of God, in this sense, derives from a much bigger cosmology than that of anthropocentric modernity. Even if they slay tyrants and killers, they are ultimately beholden to the recognition that life itself is sacred, in all its human and non-human forms. As Badrinath's translation of a verse from the Mahabharata says:

> Everyone loves one's life, and everyone receives affection from others. Even birds and beasts look at their children with eyes of affection. (p. 124)

Even if not all films emphasize its virtue uniformly, and even if it is only among several virtues exemplified by the avatars, it may indeed be possible to interpret ahimsa as the greatest dharma that is advocated in Hindu thought. Thus, even if the epics contain episodes of tremendous violence, the moral imperative ultimately is aimed at its reduction. The 'Adi Kavi', or primeval poet, Valmiki, is believed to have composed his first shloka spontaneously out of grief upon witnessing a bird killed by a hunter's arrow. It may therefore, perhaps, be said that even the greatest of the tales of the gods, the epics themselves, begin as an expression of protest against the perpetration of himsa. Within that vision, God has to stand for the good of all.

God, Devotion, Real Life

God may be the repository of the noblest of ideals, but which of these came into play when audiences watched the mythological films is a pertinent question, and a scarcely explored one in media studies. We may now have at least three generations of people in India who have seen the ancient tales of the gods come to light in the modern media, and numerous questions about what these films mean and have meant for them. At the outset, there is no doubt about the strength of appeal that mythology has had in cinema, and more recently in television. The following descriptions of audience reactions to mythology in the media capture some aspects of this:

> The thousands that flocked to see *The Birth of Shri Krishna* filmed [*sic*] at the Wellington Cinema yesterday and the day before testify to the very deep religious feeling that underlies Hindu life. The deep love for Shri Krishna that abides in the South is evinced in the atmosphere charged with emotion at the Wellington, where thousands that gather are intensely moved by the show (from *New India*, 20 January 1919, quoted in Stephen Hughes, 2005).

> In many homes the watching of Ramayana has become a religious ritual and the television set is . . . garlanded, decorated with sandalwood paste and vermillion and conch shells are blown. Grandparents admonish youngsters to bathe before the show and housewives put off serving meals so that the family is purified and fasting before Ramayan (Lavina Melwani, 1988, quoted in Philip Lutgendorf, p. 224).

These two examples of how viewers approached the tales of the gods have much in common, but are from different periods of India's history. The first example describes the response in 1920s' Madras to Phalke's film *The Birth of Shri Krishna*. The second example, from the 1980s, evokes the ritualistic devotion with which viewers across India took to the nationally televised serial *Ramayan*. In all the cases, the fact that mythology is approached as something more than just entertainment is not in doubt. There is a certain amount of reverence, religiosity even, in how mythology has been viewed. At the same time, the historic contexts in which these

examples are taking place are important too. Phalke's films
were being watched when the freedom struggle was gathering
momentum and Gandhian values had widespread resonance.
Ramayan was being watched in the 1980s, in a new, domestic
medium, surrounded by the early signs of commercialism
and consumer culture everywhere, as well as the ascension of
religious nationalism to centre stage in Indian politics. While
the political implications of these examples may be different,
there is one important common thread underlying them—
the stories of the gods are not seen by viewers as mere stories.
The gods, in a sense, are real to their viewers.

Das Gupta (2008) writes that when cinema began in India,
'[t]he devout in the audience sat barefoot, entranced as if
before mobile idols, occasionally making obeisance or
offerings' (p. 50). However, it was not just the strangeness of
the new medium that evoked such awe among viewers. It was
also the fact that the new medium was presenting not just a
train arriving in a station or a wrestling match, but the gods
themselves. An image of God, whether in a temple or on a
screen, does not represent another reality in a modern sense
for the devout. When a devotee stands before the deity of
Lord Venkateshwara in Tirumala, he or she is not looking at
a 'statue' of Vishnu but the Lord himself, as the idea of
darshan would suggest (Diana Eck, 1981). Even if the cinema
hall (or living room) is not given quite the same level of ritual
sanctity as a temple, what is important for us to recognize is
that cinema (and later television) is mediating a relationship
between deity and devotee.

The 'realism' attributed to mythological cinema may have
as much to do with ways of perceiving a new visual medium,
as with the ways in which relations between humans and

gods have been understood in popular traditions. It is a question not just of faith, but of devotion. As Dwyer (2006) shows, the impact of the Bhakti movement across the Indian subcontinent cannot be overlooked in a discussion of how viewers approach the divine in cinema. Bhakti stresses a personal and emotional relationship with God as opposed to ritualistic or intellectual approaches. It is personal in the sense that the divine is approached by the devotee in a number of ways—as a friend, as a parent, as a servant and so on—as we can see in the tales of Krishna and Arjuna, or Rama and Hanuman, for example. It is emotional in the sense the divine is understood essentially through a process of surrendering to one's feelings about it. Emotion, in a sense, is the touchstone for the validity of experience in Bhakti. If one does not feel, then whatever one says about God becomes mere ritualism, devoid of real devotion.

It may not be out of place to talk about an epistemology of emotion in a discussion of Indian cinema in general and mythological and devotional films in particular. As Owen Lynch (1990) writes, emotions are often seen in Western, modern epistemologies in psychobiological terms, as somehow less authentic than a real, intellectual or rational self. For example, we say someone 'breaks down' when he or she is showing emotions. However, in the context of Indian everyday life, especially in the terrain of religious experience, emotions are paramount. It is perhaps only through honesty in emotion that we can understand ourselves and others accurately, and ethically. In the case of mythological cinema, we can see the relevance of emotions at various levels—in depictions of how the gods and their companions feel about each other in the context of their relationships; in how and how much their devotees feel for them (especially in the saint films, but also in the depiction of devotees in mythologicals); and most of all in how they are experienced, understood and brought into meaning by their audiences. Even in the earliest Indian silent films, we see examples of what Dwyer calls the 'aesthetics of astonishment'. Whether it is in the reactions to special-effect miracles or through other iconic moments in the epics—such as Krishna dancing on top of the river serpent Kaliya—the films also invoke devotion from ordinary people within their stories and imagery.

Where does this sort of emotion, both in the text and in the audience's engagement with it, take the mythological in the real world? Ideally, the role of emotion in art may be understood in terms of the rasa theory as leading the 'individual emotional states of the spectators into a single emotional field' (Lewis Rowell, 1992, p. 328). The process of communication in this approach may be summarized not as a mere transmission of information rooted in codes of realism and rational practicality, but as an overall emotional experience that arises from a relational narrative; leading to a heightened emotional social experience which, within an ethical imperative and ultimately, leads to a proper understanding of things—towards satya and dharma, as it were. The devotee, of course, lives in the real world of history, both in the broader and in the personal sense. His or her engagement with mythological or devotional cinema also takes place within the ideologies of the time. It is not surprising perhaps, then, that the mythological has come to be associated in Indian political history with two rather strikingly different ideologies, in different times.

If we examine the context of the times in which mythological and devotional cinema began its career, we find that the films resonated with the nationalist struggle at various levels—and it was not so much with the Hindu nationalist ideology that began to emerge from some quarters at this time, but with the much more universal and egalitarian Gandhian nationalism, which was itself rooted in a universal understanding of Hinduism. The stories of the gods not only functioned as allegories for the political realities of the time, but also sometimes served the practical function of evading the colonial censor. In at least one incident, the British authorities sought to crack down on a film because of the perceived resemblance between one of its characters, Vidura, and Gandhi. More directly, though, the stories of the saints resonated with the reformist spirit of an age when the influence of Gandhi, Ambedkar and numerous other social critics, reformers or revolutionaries was easily felt and politically mobilized. Dwyer writes, 'the devotional rose to such prominence during the 1930s when ... Gandhian nationalism was at its height' (p. 69).

Although Mahatma Gandhi rather famously disliked films, the films of the time followed him, or at least some of his sensibilities, quite sincerely. Gandhi, as Bhikhu Parekh (2001) writes, saw God as one formless entity (as truth, to be precise) open to comprehension from multiple paths, whether of 'organized' faiths or otherwise. Gandhi's view of God reasserts the primacy of one principle, although allowing for the existence of different approaches to it: 'Truth has no form. Therefore, everyone will form such an idea or image of Truth as appeals to him, and there will be as many images of Truth as there are men' (quoted in Anand Hingorani, 1998, p. 43). Gandhian universalism and that of the saint films did not contradict one another. The idea of Ishwar and Allah both being names of the same Truth was perhaps quite widely felt at the time, in cinema and in real life.

It is perhaps not surprising that the mythological and devotional films of the Gandhian period had little in common with the sort of political reaction that many scholars believe the TV versions of the epics provoked in the 1980s. As Dwyer writes, the religious films made by the famous Prabhat banner in the early twentieth century 'show a much closer connection to Ranade's reformism and Gandhi's quest for national unity than any forms of Hindu nationalism' (p. 84). The message of universalism, equality and reform permeated not only mythology and saint films, but also some of the social films of the era. When mythologicals looked like they were not serving such a purpose, there was criticism. As the following editorial from *Talk-a-Tone* magazine (1944) says:

> Mythological subjects have become the mania of the modern day film producers of our land . . . such pictures in so great numbers cannot serve any purpose or help the nation or its people at this time of the day when reason and research are the guiding principles. (p. 7)

Although the mythological genre and its Gandhian context changed after Independence, the stories of the gods remained an important feature of the media. The Golden Age of the mythological came about in Telugu in the 1950s and '60s, where it remained an A-list genre until at least the 1970s, despite the rise of other genres. The Tamil mythological too remained a popular genre in the same period. In Hindi, the mythological became a B- and even C-grade genre, drawing perhaps only the truest of believers for their ability to put faith over aesthetic consideration. However, the television revival of the mythological since the 1980s of course was a national phenomenon, and its significance is best discussed separately (I turn to this in Chapter Three). Here, it may be sufficient to say one thing though—the impact of mythology in general, and in modern media and popular culture in particular, far exceeds its association with the rise of Hindu nationalism, as much academic writing on the subject seems to imply. The connection between *Ramayan* on TV and the BJP in politics, as Dwyer says, was less a case of cause-and-effect than merely a successful attempt by the party's leadership to capitalize on it.

Since globalization and the media boom of the 1990s, new forms of the mythological and the devotional are appearing in cinema and television. After a hiatus of nearly two decades, the Telugu film industry has again begun to make mythology-related films. The focus, though, has shifted from the epics and the famous gods to more localized deities and mother goddesses, as evident in films like *Ammoru* (1995). There is also a predilection with demigods and comedy in more recent Telugu cinema. Some of the most popular films are 'socio-fantasies' featuring Yama, the lord of death. There is a cynicism about the gods, too, that appears often. In a recent film, also titled *Maya Bazar*, Kubera, the demigod of wealth, is sent to present-day earth to free himself from a terrible situation—he has fallen sick after accepting all the ill-gotten wealth donated by pilgrims with bad consciences at the famous Venkateshwara temple in Tirumala. Finally, it is important to note that at least two of the most popular recent films in Telugu, *Annamayya* (1997) and *Sri Ramadasu* (2006), are saint films. It is worth pointing out, despite being the unsurpassed leader of mythological and devotional cinema in India (and perhaps the world too), the state of Andhra Pradesh is hardly a bedrock for religious extremism.

Another form in which mythology has reappeared in recent times is animation, aimed largely at the first generation of children born in India since liberalization and their diasporic cousins. How audiences will negotiate the meaning of God in these new forms and stories, in a very different context from those of early mythological cinema, remains to be seen. Will children start to see Hanuman—now with his surfer styles and American mannerisms—as just another superhero like Superman? Or will some other meanings also prevail? In some ways, the fusion of contemporary themes with popular representations of God is not unusual in India. Ganesha has appeared with everything from cellular phones to cricket bats in his hands. In 2007, a Durga Puja pandal in Kolkata nearly got the wrong end of a Quidditch stick when its *Harry Potter* theme raised the copyright bogey. The forms in which God is being reimagined are diverse and eclectic. However, these are not the only ways in which religiosity may be being reworked to suit a changing world.

The relationship between God and Indians these days seems to be shaped by both capitalism and democracy. As Pavan Varma (2004) writes, people deal with God the way they deal with different political parties. If one does not deliver, they pray to another one. They make deals and they expect things— good marks, jobs, foreign visas, marriage matches—and will carry out their vows accordingly. While this may seem somewhat mercenary, the fact is that, even with globalization, there has been no decline in the pervasiveness of God in the media or in everyday life. Everyone may not stop what they are doing and pray every time they see an image of a god on TV as they might have done before, since these images are now ubiquitous; but temples are still seen as sacred, even if tourism and commerce sometimes confuse the spiritual and the recreational.

Most importantly, the 'myths' are not regarded as mere stories at all. Even with the rise of scientific education, religion has not been abandoned as mere superstition. Instead, there is the opposite tendency—to try and view the stories of the gods through not just the feeling of devotion, but with the certitudes of science and history as well. In the summer of 2007, a proposal to dredge a canal through the land mass known as Adam's Bridge between India and Sri Lanka met with outrage when the Archaeological Survey of India testified that there was no proof that this was indeed 'Rama Setu' or the bridge built by Lord Rama's soldiers. There may have been political interests at work in this controversy, but there is also no denying the fact that what we often dismiss—with the arrogance of modernity—as mere 'belief' is deep and wide in India; and, sometimes, it is used not just for destruction, as critics point out, but also for protection. (The environmental fallout of this canal was expected to be severe.) If there is one less tree fallen or one less fish killed, perhaps there is no harm in this so-called 'literary character' named Rama (as the Archaeological Survey of India seemed to suggest) being thought of as God.

How India understands God in its media and popular culture may be seen, from one perspective, as a continuing negotiation between the modern and the non-modern. Among the non-modern sensibilities, we find many of the elements that informed the Gandhian view of religion. We see a universalism, a sense of emotional surrender, relational . obligation and aesthetic sensibility. In the modern approach, we see both the better side of modern values like egalitarianism and social mobility, as well as its tyrannies like anthropocentrism, identity politics and, of course, violence. As Lawrence Babb and Susan Wadley (1995) show, the media and modernity have freed God from the shackles of pre-modern politics to some extent. Old sectarian borders have fallen, as different gods come together in posters, serials, films and the lives of people. The upward mobility of whole communities since Independence, which I address further in later chapters, has ensured that God no longer remains the exclusive domain of any feudal sort of hierarchy. There are, of course, new forms of exclusionary thinking afoot that play out on larger scales than ever before—national in scope, scientific in ambition, driven by money and power. But, in their exclusionary-ness, these trends of thought are not God; merely politics. Meanwhile, the encounter between God and modernity has also spread itself in ways that sustain the views of God associated with the popular sentiments of cinema audiences. Modern gurus like Sri Sathya Sai Baba and Amma reach out to devotees across class, caste and regional divides, and embody and extol the virtues of universalism, ahimsa and all the good things one can imagine. For the more Westernized middle and upper classes, there are new-age gurus like Deepak Chopra, who can always turn one good thing into another. In any form, it seems, God stays.

The challenge, though, is whether we recognize Him, in whatever name, form or absence thereof. That recognition is itself recognized in Indian popular culture as an important thing. We may not know for certain whether the idealized views of God we see in films are what prevail for everyone, everywhere, in an age when a mercenary, selfish approach to the self and others is widely seen as requisite, not just for success, but even for survival. But one consolation may be drawn from the fact that, while the popular practice of religion in India may be unreflective and even ritualistic, as Varma observes, the views of God that underlie it are enlightened and sometimes do serve the people in unexpected spiritual ways. Popular religion in India has not always been a highly self-aware one, and that may be one reason why it is so easily branded, whether by right-wing political groups or left-wing academics. But recognition is important in Indian cinema and life, and not merely because we are status-obsessed. As I show in the next chapter, our films celebrate recognition as a pivotal moment in the narrative—the long-lost brothers must find each other; Hindu and Muslim and Christian must recognize they are brothers in the eyes of India and under God; the good daughter-in-law must be exonerated before her selfish mother-in-law. Ultimately, it is truth that our films say we must recognize.

God, too, finds His recognition from time to time in Indian life in ways that belie the trappings of ritual and pomp. It is, once again, not about recognizing the one true God over the false gods or anything so base, but about apprehending realities that are deeper—that God is one; that all life is bound together and sacred; that violence is unnecessary; that life is sad; that nothing is real; that this world goes on within and without us; that what goes around comes around; that everything is everything; that wonder and awe can teach us more than word or threat. It is not surprising, perhaps, that Krishna is the avatar whose stories most frequently abound with issues of (mis)recognition. His greatest moments are those in which he dispels all such doubts. Living in human form in the midst of great political struggles on the cusp of the Kali Yuga, Krishna is not above the problem of slander and calumny. He has to show himself as divine, frequently. Sometimes, as a child, it is innocent—for example, when he opens his mud-chewing mouth to his mother to reveal the whole cosmos. Mostly, it is out of grave necessity. When Krishna goes to the Kaurava court as an ambassador to try and prevent the war, the vile princes try to capture him. In a flash, he reveals himself to be not of human constraints. The elders recognize and bow to him, even though they are bound by their complex duties and obligations to fight against him in the coming war. Finally, on the eve of the great battle, as Arjuna hesitates and Krishna begins his great admonition the Bhagavad Gita, he reveals his cosmic form, the Vishwa Roopa to Arjuna (which, in a situation all too common like the supposed laundry after the enlightenment, is duly forgotten by Arjuna later and leads him to ask, a few days after the war, 'What was that stuff you told me on the battlefield, I can't recall?').

But Krishna is felt and recognized every day in this life— sometimes by the name of God, sometimes by the names of humans and sometimes with no name at all. Such a moment is beautifully narrated by Paul William Roberts (1996) in his travelogue, as he bids farewell to the India he loves one more time from his plane. Watching the features of the land disappear as a wailing Urdu ghazal plays on the headphones, Roberts offers an aching sense of love for the country he can neither live with or without, an aching sense of love, indeed, for this world:

And I have presumed, from love and casual regard,
    Called you Krishna, Yadava, and friend,
    Thinking you a friend, forgetting who you are.
I have lowered you in laughter, resting, eating,
    And waking alone and in company,
Forgive me, Krishna.

For you are the Father of the World . . .

—The Bhagavad Gita

2

COUNTRY

Devdas
Jagte Raho
Jis Desh Mein Ganga Behti Hain
Sholay
Amar Akbar Anthony
Deewar
Don

IT IS SOMETIMES SAID THAT IN A COUNTRY AS DIVERSE AS INDIA, THERE are only two cultural pastimes that can claim a pan-Indian reach—cricket and cinema. In the days before satellite television, the Internet and mobile phones, there was indeed a sweeping pervasiveness to the sight of men huddled around transistor radios listening to the live commentary as India played England or the West Indies, their bodies converging and rising in accompaniment to the crescendos in the commentator's voice signifying boundaries or dismissals. For a long time before cricket morphed into a multicolour, brand-infested TV spectacle for youthful patriots who painted the Indian flag on their cheeks (and often turned India–Pakistan matches into symbolic but sometimes deadly machismo contests between Hindus and Muslims), a slightly less in-your-face (literally) sense of the nation was what perhaps lay in popular notions of what it meant to be an Indian, and much of this sensibility came from cinema. The vitality and centrality of our films to our sense of ourselves as a nation is not in doubt. Ramachandra Guha (2007), after all, takes over 800 eloquent pages to illustrate his opening point (just how many and how divided we are), and then concludes with at least one reassuring historian's prophecy: India will survive as long as, among other things, its films are watched and songs are sung.

What is it, though, about our films that makes them so closely tied in with a sense of who we are as a nation? Is it only

the fact that cinema has a vast common reach in a country
with no common language, or is there something that can be
said about the predilections of popular cinema as well that
makes it a truly national cultural form? What are the stories,
which our films have told, about what it means to be Indian?
India, in one sense, has been made as much by the meanings
it has been given in cinema as it has by the common national
form of the cinema, or the politics and history beyond them.
The evolution of Indian cinema has paralleled that of India
very closely, starting from the period of anti-colonial
nationalism, through the Nehruvian era of nation-building,
and into the present period of globalization as well. In each of
these contexts, popular cinema has not only represented,
through its own idiomatic ideals, the daily lives and concerns
of people, but has also frequently commented explicitly on
what the country means, or ought to mean to us. In this
sense, 'Country' has perhaps been as big a predilection for
Indian cinema as 'God'. There are certainly numerous
instances of films and songs in which devotion to country is
exhorted on the same level, and often in the same form, as
devotion to God. However, there is one important
difference—cinema borrowed from past traditions in
performance and philosophy in its vision of God for modern
audiences; however, the India of cinema, much like the India
of reality, was from the beginning, an imagined one.

Imagined India

To get to the heart of Sunil Khilnani's (1999) important
question, 'Who is an Indian?' we could begin by asking the
question of 'What is India?' Is it a territory? A tradition? A
civilization? A people? These questions and more have of

course been expressed in lofty words and with beautiful music in many film songs over the last century. However, since India was created not by films alone, but by the politics that preceded, sustained and, as Khilnani would say, 'constituted' it, it may be useful to outline the contexts in which cinema gave voice to popular ideas about what it means to be a nation. To begin with, the idea of India, in its present form or even approximations thereof, is a fairly recent one. Even if we acknowledge the civilizational continuities that allow us to indeed speak of something called 'our' heritage that has existed for millennia before, the India that formally began its existence on 15 August 1947 is the outcome of a more immediate past, and a rather arbitrary one at that. In this sense, India was 'invented' even before it was 'discovered'. As Sudipta Kaviraj (1992) writes:

> India, the objective reality of today's history, whose objectivity is tangible enough for people to try to preserve, to destroy, to uphold, to construct and dismember, the reality taken for granted in all attempts in favour and against, is not an object of discovery, but invention. It was historically instituted by the nationalist imagination of the nineteenth century.

The nationalist imagination, of course, was dominated by its leaders. As Khilnani writes, the leaders of India's nationalist movement, such as Gandhi, Nehru, Ambedkar and Patel, had to envision modernity in Indian terms. Their vision of what India would be arose from the peculiarities of their own engagement with the broader social and philosophical implications of modernity. In the India and the cinema that came to be, we continue to see the shadow of some of their ideals. If the nationalist leaders of colonial India wrestled—

whether under the muzzle of the infamous Macaulay Minute or in other ways—the alien categories of European thought into various Indian forms of modernity, they were by no means isolated from the people while doing so. The impact of modernity was writ large in the creation of India. It was not merely in terms of the importing of new technologies and laws from England that India and Indian modernity began. It was as much in the spread of new ways of seeing, especially in new ways of seeing large, and extending power and control over everything that was being seen thus; as illustrated perhaps by the 'census, map and museum' that Kaviraj talks about.

If the material reality of India arose somewhere in the negotiation between colonial rule and the nationalist elites, the popular sensibilities of being Indian were of course not outside the purview of modernity either. It is in this context that the role of media in general becomes relevant. The nation is a modern idea. It entails the amassing of vast populations across traditional boundaries of language, religion and custom into a singular entity whose existence is premised not only on the trappings of power such as the state, but also on the construction of a consciousness that fundamentally becomes shared by people across time and space. As Benedict Anderson's (1991) famous notion of 'imagined communities' implies, mass media audiences become aware, by virtue of their consumption of media, that there may be other people just like them, even if these people are distant strangers whom they will probably never meet, who are also consuming the same media and perhaps having similar feelings and experiences. Anderson shows how this happened in Europe soon after the invention of the printing press. When people began to read certain novels, they were able to imagine themselves for the first time as part of a greater collectivity than their local communities. It is from such 'imagined communities' that nationalism arose as a modern phenomenon.

By the time Phalke made *Raja Harischandra* in 1913, the idea of Indian independence was fairly well under way. Phalke's own inspiration was very much nationalistic. His interest in cinema was fired by a desire to bring India's own gods to life on the screen, after watching a film about Christ. In a few years, the new medium of cinema had captivated audiences in India. While many people approached it as a sacred experience, the Indian elite, who had already been at the vanguard of the demand for home rule, saw the possibility for 'imagined community' that mythological cinema represented.

However, despite the political promise Phalke's mythologicals had presented following their screening in South India, the proliferation of films in the next decade dissipated such a possibility, according to Hughes (2005). The Indian Independence movement by this time had very much coalesced around the figure of Mahatma Gandhi. It is no surprise, then, that the screening of *Bhakta Vidur* in Madurai created grave concerns for British officials, who saw the wise Vidura as a stand-in for Gandhi, and the blind Dhritarashtra as none other than King George. Even though the films of this period did not directly serve as a rallying point for a nationalistic imagined community, they clearly followed Gandhi's lead. As Hughes points out, the mythologicals did not present the stories of the gods as something with mere heritage value, but sought to bring forward their relevance to the present. They functioned as 'a way of using Hindu religious and moral truths as vehicles for modern social reform and uplift' (p. 229). It is, however, in the period after the 'social' became the main genre of Indian cinema that we can begin to examine a closer relationship between the concerns of cinema and the nation that was being born all around it. Even if India formally became independent in 1947, the idea of India continues to be an ongoing creation—not only in politics, but as much in the daily lives of its people, who see at least some part of what we hope to see in ourselves as a nation in our films.

In the following pages, I examine exactly what some of these hopes were in the popular films of the post-mythological era. I focus on three broad themes which I think represent a more or less chronological sequence in which popular cinema has evolved, and situate them where appropriate in the broader social context. I begin with a section titled 'Mother', in which I look at the strange predilections of some of the early social films of the 1930s and '40s, the most famous of which would be *Devdas* (1935). In the following section, 'Motherland', I look at the period that many people consider the Golden Age of Indian cinema, the 1950s and '60s. In this section, I show how popular Hindi cinema, best represented by the films of Raj Kapoor, expressed the dreams and disappointments of the newly born India of Nehru. In the last section, 'Land', I turn to the 1970s and the rise of the 'Angry Young Man' genre, symbolized, of course, by Amitabh Bachchan. Finally, I also consider one important question that has bothered scholars of cinema and nationalism: Why realism has somehow been less important in popular cinema than recognition, usually of something we could call 'truth'.

Mother (1930s–50s)

The figure of the mother has loomed larger than that of perhaps any other character in Indian cinema. It may have been a prophetic start that in the very first scene of India's very first film, *Raja Harischandra*, what we see is the queen and her aides fussing over the prince in a display of matter-of-fact maternal solicitude. Since then, the mother has become not only an important figure in the narrative, but virtually the reigning deity of whatever idealism Indian cinema has aspired to. From the classic *Mother India* of the 1950s, through various action films dedicated to 'Maa' in the 1970s, and even in the unlikely context of a terrorist drama in 1999, the mother has figured as the guiding principle for how our films would like the world to function. During this time, the figure of the mother drew on a number of different sensibilities, ranging from the devotional (in films about the mother goddess, for example) to the everyday (mother as avenger). The mother, of course, was also important in another form— as Bharat Mata. There is no dearth of tableaux-like songs featuring a map of India and Bharat Mata marching forth from it, astride a lion. Given the enduring importance of the mother in our cinema, it may be helpful to begin a study of the national ideal under her auspices. Of course, one dare not directly ask the question of what the mother means in Indian cinema, simply because that is a matter perhaps for a whole book (or twenty). In this section, though, I am interested in exploring not so much the mother herself (as goddess, nation or just flesh-and-blood mother), but in what was perhaps the first archetypal hero of popular Indian cinema—the proverbial mother's boy.

The first archetypal hero of Indian cinema (apart from

Lord Krishna, of course) was not just a mama's boy, but, to
use Nandy's (2001) memorable phrase, a 'terribly maudlin,
effeminate, self-destructive' mama's boy' at that. He was, in
one name that we would all recognize, Devdas. *Devdas* was
based on Sarat Chandra Chattopadhyay's 1919 Bengali novel
and made numerous times in multiple languages. The 1935
version with K.L. Saigal is especially renowned because of his
singing and the shadow of his own persona on the story.
While the story speaks of unrequited love, drinking and
tragedy, we also see in the film numerous signs of India's
encounters with early-twentieth-century modernity even if
that modernity seems as inconspicuous as a small mailbox in
the song 'Piya Bin', for instance. But it is in the character
himself that we see perhaps the greatest and tortured signs of
a certain part of India's encounter with modernity. While
Devdas's great unrequited love and melancholic and
ultimately suicidal drinking all seem like elements of the
archetypal doomed romance, we can also read it in terms of
the social history of its context.

Devdas is often interpreted as a case study of the weakness
of the declining feudal elite, especially when faced with the
daunting onslaught of the city. However, as Nandy writes, it
was not only about the 'anguish of the first generation rural
elite's encounter with the city' (p. 52), but also about a 'sense
of exile from maternal utopia' (p. 45). Devdas's exasperating
helplessness in terms of either getting what he wants, or
getting over it, has social and psychological implications.
Nandy suggests that Devdas's self-destructive longing is part
of a pattern which involves a journey from the village to the
city, and then somewhat of a thwarted journey back to the
village. This also parallels, in relational terms, a journey from

maternity to conjugality and towards maternity again. Finally, this journey may also be seen in temporal terms, as a flight from the past (village) to the present (city), only to be compelled towards a sort of lost past once again (return to village). Devdas's condition, if we may call it that, is very much part of the dilemma of modernity. Faced with loss of privilege in the world of the village, the young feudal elite flee to the city. Overcome by anonymity in the city, they seek the village once again. In a sense, as Nandy writes elsewhere, that is what we are doing when we watch Indian films too—we are seeking in its dreams the impossible return to the village. Devdas, of course, dies tragically. We, the melancholic postcolonial viewers, remain content with a vicarious experience in Saigal's voice.

To understand *Devdas* as a negotiation between the modern and non-modern, we can turn briefly to the broader context. The films of the 1930s inevitably bring up questions about the influence of Gandhi. Akbar Ahmad (1992) writes that even in action films, despite the hero being an Errol Flynn in his swashbuckling fights, in his morals he was still expected to be a Gandhian. In the case of tragic heroes like Devdas, Ahmad suggests that the helpless surrender to fate may be a form of misconstrued Gandhianism. It may be worth clarifying what the difference indeed is, in terms of the encounter of the modern and the non-modern, between Gandhi's spiritual form of surrender and Devdas's rather decadent and self-destructive one. Gandhian non-violence, for example, is often mistaken by Western observers for something they call 'passivity', which seems to imply an abject surrender to events. For Gandhi, even 'passive resistance' was not passive at all. It called for enormous

agency in terms of self-control and discipline. Surrender, in a
sense, was to a higher principle, not to any sort of immediate
or mundane provocation. For Devdas, it was perhaps a lot
less Gandhian. He surrendered, for sure. But lacking the
non-modern networks of privilege or family to surrender
into, he falls permanently into his own weak ineffectuality. In
contrast, by the 1970s, Amitabh Bachchan would define the
hero simply in terms of his 'active intervention in fate', Nandy
writes (p. 70).

If we interpret the Devdas archetype as a national symptom,
especially in the context of the colonial period, perhaps we
can see the 'lost maternal utopia' as a symbol for the nation as
well. Even though 'Bharat Mata' may not have been an
explicitly deified idea in the time of the colonial censor, the
idea of the nation as a mother was perhaps not too uncommon
in the 1930s. The tragic hero could also simply be that way
from his grief at the thought of his imprisoned mother. It
might only be coincidental, but when we compare the two
main genres from the Gandhi era—the mythological and the
social—we find that the former is happy and heavenly, and
the latter is marked by tragedies like *Devdas*. Real life was
perhaps rather painful in that sense too. The nationalist
consciousness was quite awake by this time. Perhaps the
sorrow that reeks in the cinema halls of this time is something
like that of Hamlet's upon discovering the fate of his father—
it is the feeling of waking up to a reality that cannot be
represented just yet in the cinema, but one that is felt deeply
by most Indians. It is perhaps the rage of the child who
cannot help the enslaved mother. And the mother, even
when physically absent, is still always there; and like God, she
is always good. What a burden that places on the son, especially

a maudlin one at that! In the decades following *Devdas*, even though the hero learns to take charge of his destiny, we find the equation of mother and son remaining central to the stories. It is almost in the same manner as God to his devotees, and the nation to its subjects. In time, as the self-centred individual of modernity and the omnipotent hero of cinema become more commonplace, we find that even as the mother stays important, like God, like nation, she is there only to serve the hero; not unlike the heroine too. But the mother still gets more eulogies.

Motherland (1950s–60s)

The loosely understood, if deeply felt, notion of relating to something called the nation as a child would to its mother did indeed acquire a more modern and territorial mandate that was to become a reality ultimately with Independence in 1947. The idea of a motherland was often alluded to in the films of this decade. NTR's first film was *Mana Desam* (Our nation, 1949) and shows a family's dilemmas against the wider backdrop of the freedom struggle. By the end of the 1940s, even mythology, with its heavenly settings, began to drop enough hints about the earth down below. The 1940 version of *Bhukailasa*, for example, concludes its story with a documentary-like sequence about the temples and holy places associated with the events in the film. It is a reminder, perhaps, that even though India was scarcely imagined in theocratic terms, the idea that the gods too walked this land was not altogether absent in popular cinema. In the images of the crowds of pilgrims, it is also perhaps a reminder that India is all about its people, diverse though they may be. The film itself is seen by film historians as a sign of the industry's diversity—it is a Telugu film directed by a Marathi director featuring a Kannada actor and produced by a Tamil studio magnate.

Modern independent India, of course, came to be shaped less by religion than by two important personalities who had quite different views about not just religion, but about modernity in general. Gandhi was a reasoned critic of modernity and found much of what he needed in the non-modern, even a deep faith in the common culture of humanity (though we associate universalism with the ideals of modernity rather than the non-modern). Nehru, on the other hand, was a believer in modernity and progress. He had little room for religion. By the time India became independent and began to grow into a state, it was Nehru's vision that came to prevail on India. However, in the films of this time, as we will see in this section, we see a rather non-modern sensibility shaping the actions of their characters. It is not the failed pre-modernity of declining feudals like Devdas though. It is the non-modern of Gandhi, coming to head, and to grip, with the pros and cons of Nehruvian modernity.

Nehru's vision for India included guiding principles for the state such as 'democracy, religious tolerance, economic development, and cultural pluralism' (Khilnani, 1999, p. 12). In Nehru's era, many of these came to be a reality not only in terms of the institutions of the modern state, but also in terms of a political and cultural resonance among the people which could hardly have been taken for granted. As Khilnani writes elsewhere, the idea of democracy was essentially quite alien to India. In time, it would come to rest almost entirely on the idea that people could—and would—vote. But at that time it would have to take shape and root not only because of the idealism of people like Nehru, but also because that was the only way the vast diversity of groups and interests in India could be accommodated. The ideal of religious tolerance was already quite severely tested by Partition. There were powerful leaders who did not entirely share Nehru's notions of pluralism. Moreover, as a consequence of Partition and the complex set of factors which shaped the formation of India, there were territorial issues—some like Hyderabad have since been resolved, and others like Kashmir seemingly not. The idea of India was complex enough for a state, and a disappointment for its people as the years passed, but never a cause for complete despair. The enduring legacy of Nehru, as Khilnani writes—and to some extent the cinema of this time—would be faith in the state.

In time, the state would fall from grace in the world of cinema, even as it would in real life with the Emergency and the rise and fall and rise of Indira Gandhi. However, in the 1950s, the cinematic vision of India was not anywhere close to losing faith in the nation or its institutions. It would take a long look at some of its failures and record, in its own register of intense feelings and tested relationships and hard times, the struggle of the everyman. But the struggle against injustice, tyranny and deprivation were often presented within the terms of a moral struggle. In the end, faith was re-allotted to the state for taking India forward, materially and, as it were, spiritually. In the 1950s and '60s, cinema encountered modernity and made it a little more familiar to the fundamentally non-modern moral sensibilities of its audiences. It did not diminish its engagement with either, but it generated ways of thinking about one's self and community and nation in a manner that was in equal parts

Gandhian morality and Nehruvian 'democratic idealism'
(Khilnani, 1999). As Ahmad writes:

> In the early years the ideas and values of Nehru were used
> and parodied by Bombay Heroes self-consciously, bravely,
> spoke of naia zamana, naia roshni, new age, new light. They
> spoke of pyar, love, the struggle against zulm, oppression,
> injustice, satyagraha, non-violence, shanty, peace, and
> dharma, duty. These were the key words of the new nation,
> Bharat Mata, Mother India, and they ran through the
> dialogues in the films. (p. 292)

The new day of independent India played out in a number of
ways in the films of this period. The idea of righteousness
prevailing over injustice was portrayed in the powerful form
of the classic *Mother India*, with its familiar themes of the
struggling peasant, greedy moneylender and of, course, the
all-important mother. We see the mother here not only as
the source of life and sustenance, but as the custodian of the
moral order as well. An even more literal (and upbeat)
celebration of the motherland, of course, came about a few
years later in the form of the song 'Mere Desh Ki Dharti'
(*Upkar*, 1967), with its invocations of plenty and bounty. In
the rural setting of these examples, we see shades of both
Gandhi's and Nehru's India; we see the all-important question
of morality and justice (even if it is not strictly non-violent),
and we see the popularization of the idea of thinking big, a
modern Nehruvian ideal, in the form of productivity and
harvests.

The definitive engagement with the nation in this period,
though, is perhaps what we find in the films of Raj Kapoor. In
some ways, Raj Kapoor's roles and persona embodied what
we could call the emerging India of that time. In the 1950s,

India was emerging not as a global knowledge power (as we hear these days), but really as a movement from village to nation. Its definitive image was that of the displaced, wide-eyed villager emerging from train or bus into the vast busy faceless swarm of the city. It marks the beginning of the street as the setting for Indian cinema.

However, the street was not yet the place for angry young men that it became in the subsequent era, nor was it the scene of drunken despair to be found in *Devdas*. *Devdas* is about the harsh transition from the village to the city for the declining elite, but in Raj Kapoor we see a different aspect of the same encounter, that of the less privileged but ever-so-representative common man. The street, despite its harshness, was still, in its heart, a village. Perhaps like the river waters diverted by the big dams—so symbolic in those days of progress—to service the urban population, the men and women of the village too spilled out of their distant shelters and embankments to wander into the merciless city, where they would only be drunk dry. Appropriately enough, the theme of water is at the heart of one of Raj Kapoor's most compelling roles at this time. In *Jagte Raho* (1956), a film which was not quite commercially successful but captured the essence of the common man's condition in India and in cinema, Raj Kapoor plays an innocent villager who wanders into an apartment building at night in search of water and is mistaken for a thief. In a fantastic sequence of scenes built around his hiding and fear of discovery, we find a searing critique of the false morality and corruption of the urban middle-class residents of the building even as they rustle up the equivalent of a lynch mob to hunt him down. The men and women of middle-class India in their urban nests show a callous hypocrisy in their fear of the 'thief', for behind their petty fears rest moral corruption and sanctimony. The worst of the lot, perhaps, is the supposedly reputable businessman, who is in reality running a counterfeiting operation. The chase reaches a pinnacle of sorts when the victim is forced to climb up a drainpipe to evade capture by the mob screaming from below. It is at this moment that we see him glance through a window at a picture of Jesus on the wall, suggesting the crucifixion of the innocent by the hypocritical and corrupt.

The film's melodrama is perhaps a bit more subtly constructed than in other films, forcing a feeling of helpless rage against the plight of the innocent and his all-too-human need for water. Every time he comes close to taking a sip, he is thwarted. However, there is what we would now call an 'edge' in how much and how far the seemingly (in retrospect) mildly villainous characters will go to hide their evil deeds. The incitation to violence, the lack of regard for life (a doctor is one of the villains as well), the false piety (a holy person is as crooked as the rest) and the mob, all seem symbolic of problems then and now. In spite of the relentless suffering, and the seeming despair of the situation, there is, in the end a glimmer of hope, offered by a child who accepts the 'thief' for his innocence. She reminds him that he didn't do anything bad, and he should therefore not be afraid. Finally, in the famous song sequence 'Jago Mohan Pyare', a woman played by Nargis (whom Raj Kapoor called the 'mother' of his films) turns from watering plants to pour the thirsty man his drink. Lord Krishna, it seems, has woken up to the plight of his people, at last.

Films like *Jagte Raho* and the earlier *Shree 420* (1955) were critical of what Rajni Bakshi (1998) calls the 'unfulfilled promises of Independence'. The problem was squarely seen in these films as capitalism, although the critique that was offered was by no means spoken in the language of modern socialism. Bakshi notes, aptly enough, that 'the depth of misdeed and greed (in these films) was directly proportionate to the height and size of the mansion' (p. 108). But the critique of capitalism in these stories was framed not in explicit political, economic or ideological terms, but in the universal language of emotions, relationships and morality that was more widely and deeply felt among audiences. It is even less surprising, perhaps, that Raj Kapoor was so popular in the Soviet Union. As Bakshi points out, even if his films were in a sense upholding socialism, they were different from the 'socialist-realism' of the Soviet cinema. As a Russian student quoted by Bakshi says, viewers in his country wished to see not war, but love and 'carefree happiness' (p. 105).

While I address the question of why our films prefer 'carefree happiness' to 'realism' in the last section of this chapter, suffice it to say that Raj Kapoor in some ways found a way to engage with both. Unlike either the unfailing gods or the failed maudlin heroes of earlier films, Raj Kapoor's characters found their solutions within a morality that embodied the best of both Gandhi and Nehru, of the non-modern and the modern. His films held a mirror up to the national self as it began its project of building itself against tremendous odds after colonialism and its aftermath. He was, in a sense, India; he was facing modernity in every sense; as a vagabond ('awara') he reflected to some extent its wanderings, its carefree sense. He was, in his own down-home manner, cosmopolitan, with his legendary Japani shoes and red Russi hat. He also represented something of a break that both Gandhi and Nehru would have desired. As a vagabond, he perhaps carried less of the baggage and burden of tradition and family. What he was breaking with was in a sense the less morally acceptable part of the past—the feudality of the familiar. As an 'awara', Raj Kapoor perhaps captured at least one progressive element of the project of modernity that was directly chipping away at an ossified hierarchy, which had its origins in the ancient past and acquired its present and immutable form under British colonialism. The vagabond was embodying a sensibility that Indian popular culture would long exalt—where he came from was less important than who he was and what he did. In this sense, a Nehruvian spirit of modernity was indeed awakening.

But this awakening was, of course, by no means a full transition from Gandhi to Nehru in India's sense of itself. It was rooted very much in the non-modern. Raj Kapoor's characters are in a way Gandhian in a post-Gandhian world. They may not be based on a doctrinal understanding of Gandhi, but they work only because the heartstrings they pull upon lead to a sensibility rooted in a Gandhian moral universe, after all. His conduct, actions and, most of all, his returning belief in something called the 'truth'—all evoke a non-modern morality that is sung out evocatively in the ode to a national self that is the title song in *Jis Desh Mein Ganga Behti Hai* (1960, here translated in Bakshi):

> We do not hanker for the endless more ... We are the children of the soil that bears everything ... We have learnt much from different peoples, welcomed strangers into our hearts and made them our own. (pp. 111–12)

The climactic confrontation in this film between the dacoits and the police is of course prevented from a violent end by

Raju's appeal to non-violence, which, as Bakshi points out, is less Gandhian in an abstract sense and made more so through the language of practical reason. In the end, Raju convinces the dacoits to surrender and, although some go to jail, the community is on the whole free to ride off into the 'promises of the Nehruvian dream' (p. 114). It is uncannily as if a motif from history was repeated in cinema. Gandhi gives us our roots and Nehru takes us forward. Don't lose hope, yet.

Tejaswini Ganti (2004) observes that it is the films of this period (and not the earlier silent era) that are often referred to as the Golden Age of Indian cinema. Perhaps the nostalgia is not just for the form alone, but for the precise manner in which the idealism of the non-modern and the modern came together. In the light of some of these films, Bakshi also wonders, 'Was there a humane gentleness and generosity inherent in us that, as a people, we squandered along the way?' (p. 93). In the following decades, neither the films nor India seemed particularly gentle or generous. There is still a sense of the moral universe at work even in the violent action films that would come to dominate Indian cinema, but the changes in cinema are far more sweeping, and as vivid and dramatic perhaps as the change in political culture that took place from Nehru to Indira Gandhi and her son Sanjay in particular. In the industry, they blamed colour and James Bond for the decline of our gentle past, but the changes were, of course, beyond the aesthetic alone. The journey from village to city was in a sense complete (in the films that is), and even though the mother remained an important figure both as her own self and as allegory for the nation, the focus was now less on her and more on the indubitable street skills of her avenging, worldly, anti-maudlin sons.

Land (1970s)

If the earliest films were about the heavens and the subsequent ones about the motherland, the most popular films of the 1970s were about not just land in a general sense, but specifically about the streets and slums of the city. These films also brought to the fore a new kind of hero who has often been described as the 'Angry Young Man'. He was angry about a lot of things that one could relate to—the common man could never get justice from the rich or the powerful, and the rich and the powerful of course had not a shred of morality in them. He was angry, most of all, from a sense of abandonment. He was abandoned by the country, the government and sometimes even by the mother. It is not surprising, perhaps, that one of the last mythologicals made with NTR in the 1970s was about Karna, the abandoned Pandava. Even mythology, it seemed, had to turn from its usual gods to the tales of those who had been unjustly treated. In *Dana Veera Shura Karna* (1977), NTR plays multiple roles and hits the point hard about those who had got the wrong end of the heroes' actions in the Mahabharata—Karna and Ekalavya—who fell to Krishna's trickery. It was a time when demigods and citizens felt let down.

What were the sources of this anger? To some extent, we can answer this question by turning to the changes in the broader political culture that took place from the 1960s onwards. The Nehruvian era may not have ended completely with his passing away in 1964, but the rise of Indira Gandhi in time did signal many political transformations in India. Despite electoral and military successes in the years to come, her regime came to be characterized by the early 1970s with a hard cynicism. For the first time, power became a singular pursuit in itself without the broader sort of vision that leaders like Gandhi and Nehru had brought to it. The Congress party, as Khilnani (1999) writes, quickly turned into an 'unaudited company for winning elections' and became less about substance and more about theatre (p. 45). In order to make up for its ideological decline, Indira Gandhi allowed herself to be projected as 'an 'individual object of adulation, identification and trust' (p. 45), thereby also becoming the 'object of all frustration and disaffection'. It was this sort of disaffection that came to characterize India's young and poor. As Fareeduddin Kazmi (1998) points out, 'unemployment and inflation were on the rise and the standard of living was falling . . . in Bombay nearly one-third of the population lived in slums or on pavements' (p. 139).

There were enough disappointments in the realities of daily life to warrant the rise of a new kind of hero, one who would wear neither his heart on his sleeve nor a smile on his face. Although the late 1960s had seen a brief period in which a romantic hero ruled, best represented by Rajesh Khanna, the new realities demanded a more aggressive representation. The new hero would, like many of his fans in the audience, not have even the luxury of a vagabond's life. His lot was the street; even there his place was unstable, fought over every day with hands and feet and, naturally, an indomitable heart (the wellsprings of which we shall read more about shortly). Unlike anyone before him, the hero was a fighter, and even a killer. That hardly tainted him though, because even at the beginning of the story, his own life has usually been destroyed by villainy of a most murderous kind, making his own vendetta somehow justifiable. In the end, as the promises of India to provide security and justice and even a decent living for its young men faded, there was no other way, the films seemed to say, but to take power into one's hand and fight, even kill.

The hero, in these films, was frequently the underdog. His professions, to begin with, were those of the working class. Kazmi (1998) notes that in many of his famous films of the 1970s, Amitabh Bachchan's characters were from the slum and the street—the dock worker, the petty crook, the waiter, the coolie, the horse-cart driver. In some films, he rises to something powerful, like a leader or an underworld boss. But he begins inevitably in the world of the masses, those whom popular cinema chose to serve, over the elites and the critics. Appropriately enough, there was a shift in aesthetic emphasis in these films as well. It was no longer the face or the eyes that carried the weight of performance, but the body as a whole. As Sumita Chakravarty (1993) notes, Amitabh Bachchan's physical features, especially his height, were used to accentuate the persona that was built around him. The hero becomes larger than life at this time, and his opening scenes begin with a reverence that even the gods may not have received in the old films—we see his feet first, and then we look up, all the way up, as if what we are looking at is not the coolie, but a giant of a man.

The Angry Young Man was fundamentally about revenge. In *Zanjeer* (1973)—the film that more or less inaugurated Amitabh Bachchan's career as one—a young boy is haunted by the sight of his family's murder (and the dangling wristband of the perpetrator with its nightmarish white horse) and grows up to become the upright police officer who gets back at the villain. In *Sholay* (1975)—the legendary 'masala western'—the vendetta may not have quite been that of the two young protagonists themselves, but their mission is fundamentally to carry out their retainer's quest for revenge. (To be fair, as the moral universe of even the vigilante genre demands, the act of violence is carried out not just for revenge, but for universal justice and security—the infamous bandit Gabbar Singh has not only slaughtered the retainer's family but continues to terrorize the innocent villagers). In these films, vendetta and violence are perhaps not so much about the sadistic pleasure of violence as a grudging recognition that the crimes inflicted on the good men and women of the nation by its increasingly pervasive villains (who are also increasingly in positions of power) can no longer be contested through Gandhian spirituality or Nehruvian police and courts. They are about just rewards and, as Kazmi writes, the scenes in which a hitherto-unassailable villain is brought down by the hero 'provide massive emotional satisfaction to the audience' (p. 142). In a society in which class divisions are clear and steep and increasingly intolerable, the class representations of hero and villain are also clearly etched in the films. The hero is a hard-working, exploited, aggrieved, sometimes even orphaned, man. The villain is rich, powerful and beyond the reach of the law. Violence, like the gun in Western folklore, is indeed the equalizer.

The moral universe built on the noblesse oblige of the older period was clearly unsustainable in cinema and in real life by this time, and a sense of rage is indeed palpable. There are certainly parallels in real life, with some of the excesses of the Emergency, as well as the violent law and order issues that started to proliferate in the years after it. However, as Kazmi asks, 'How angry is the Angry Young Man?' What is the nature of the 'rebellion' he embodies? There is clearly class inequality in the picture, and there is increasingly recourse to violence. There is also a newer and broader definition of morality at play here, not in the least in the quick and almost spontaneous withdrawal of any sort of a moral taboo on violence. Where does this rebellion go? It is tempting certainly to remember, in the context of this question, that the 1970s are also the time that Indian cinema begins to become flush with money of all sorts, especially the proverbial 'black money'. It is a much bigger enterprise and the productions show it, and show off too. After all, the villains being smugglers made it easy for the display of all sorts of desirable foreign objects such as push-button telephones and the legendary Vat 69 bottles. As Lalit Vachani (2005) notes, the financing priorities changed as well around this time, with the main star receiving as much as a third of the entire film's budget. Did the money corrupt the otherwise revolutionary sentiment of the angry young working-class hero's revolt against the corrupt elites?

From a critical perspective, as Kazmi suggests, it would seem so. The films always pull back from the class-based moral position they begin with. The hero is working class, but hardly ever works in the film. He lives a life of a status slightly above the reach of his peers. His solutions are ultimately about individual superman-like action and not about any kind of collective change. He kills the villain because his grouse is always with the bad individual, not so much with the system. In spite of his run-ins with the now-frequent figure of the corrupt cop, he has to redeem himself in the end for having been violent or an outlaw by turning himself in to the law (as any Nehruvian-era hero would) or even by sacrificing his own life (as any of the skewed satyagrahis of an even earlier time would). He also depends, for his moral and physical strength, on an unending supply of benediction from at least two sources, both of which bear out the continuities with earlier films—God and his mother. Sometimes, he needs one to save the other. In his famous temple talk in *Deewar* (1975), for example, Amitabh Bachchan concedes that he has been too cynical, but is here now to seek God's help for his mother.

The Angry Young Man may be an outsider, but he is not a loner. He may be shy, reserved, pensive, brooding, quiet, but he is anchored in a web of relationships. In *Sholay*, Amitabh Bachchan is reserved but not alone; he is, in fact, quite expressive in the display of brotherly camaraderie in the famous buddy song 'Yeh Dosti'. Even if he is orphaned, as the Angry Young Man usually is, a rude sojourn on the sidewalks is often ameliorated by the eventual finding of a family of sorts. Sometimes, he picks up children who have nowhere to go, as in *Don* (1978), and takes care of them. In time, he will of course also develop a relationship of sorts with a romantic lead, but none of these parallels his relationship with his mother. In films like *Deewar*, Vachani (2005) writes, the hero's story may well be the quest of an outsider, but it is rooted in the perception of a rejection by the mother in favour of a brother who happens to be on the right side of the law. On the other hand, there is also the abiding theme of the long-lost brother. Numerous films of this time deal with the topic of children separated from their families (usually by the acts of a violent villain), who go through numerous twists and turns to not only reunite finally, but to recognize each other for who they are. The theme of long-lost brothers reuniting, usually on the basis of a serendipitous observation that might well have been obvious to the audience for all three hours, has made the locket or amulet or talisman placed by the mother an icon of some jest and parody as well. In the late 1990s, a promo for a global television channel features three such long-lost brothers recognizing each other by the fragments of the talisman they have. The three pieces are 'M', 'T' and 'V'.

In the 1970s though, the three separated brothers were of course best known as Amar, Akbar and Anthony (from *Amar Akbar Anthony*, 1977). There is hope in their story that— despite the failings of the state and the rise of the violent hero—at least the spirit of universalism and brotherhood, preferably under the auspices of a national mom, will persist and prevail. Such a spirit, of course, is not so much analysed as felt. The emphasis on emotions remains as strong as ever, even if these are placed increasingly in the service of elaborate action sequences rather than songs alone, as in the past. Even as the 'body' became a dominant motif in the cinema of the 1970s, particularly in fights and dances, the eyes were still used to signify emotions, as Chakravarty writes:

> In direct contrast to his body, however, are the semiotics of Bachchan's eyes. Heavy-lidded, slightly deep-set . . . his eyes are the most striking feature of his face . . . [and] register a whole range of emotions . . . against a backdrop of pathos and unspoken sadness. (p. 229)

The violence of the action film was in some ways absorbed into the emotional language of the melodrama and, deeper yet, into the relational moral universe which still lay at the heart of the popular cinema of this time. It would obviously not have sufficed for an Indian audience if the hero merely took to the gun to settle his problem with the evil villain. A cold, unfeeling vigilante would perhaps have been too much of a break from a cultural sensibility rooted in the gods, saints and Gandhi. His situation in a difficult time has demanded violence of him—there are no jobs, no protection from villains, and money is more easily made on the wrong side of the law. In a nation waking up to its failures after a steady run on hope, there is perhaps not enough spirit or wisdom to take on such a reality without the tempting solution of violence. Within the industry too, there is the sense of competition, of the need to expand on stunts and gore. The desires of a mass for whom the slum and the street are realities with little chance of escape perhaps warrant such a hero who will not leave the villains alone until he is duly avenged.

However, the hero also has to come back to the fold of the nation, and to the broad ways of knowing and feeling that underpin its value structures. This has been done in these films in a number of ways. Sometimes, the hero surrenders to the police and pays his dues for having taken the law into his own hands. Sometimes, a double is introduced, as in the case of the ever-popular Don. The villainous Don is a criminal and the innocent lookalike sent in to impersonate him can thus absolve himself of his conduct (like drinking) by appealing to the audience's knowledge that it is not really him. Finally, there is always the option of sacrifice. The hero who has carried a lifetime of suffering inside him for lost parents and unreciprocated loves can always sacrifice himself. In *Muqaddar ka Sikandar* (1978), Amitabh Bachchan suffers excruciatingly for his own losses and his childhood sweetheart. 'What use is it to live without you, o friend?' he sings. But the friend is in love with another friend, and there are many, many complications in the situation. The hero has also risen— on the strength of a holy man's prophecy—from his dismal lot on the sidewalk to riches and power. Like *Devdas* decades before, even the superstar hero of the 1970s faces the problem of the unattainable woman. In the end, there is a real villain he must kill, even if he has to give his own life to do so. He does. The audience leaves in tears.

Realism and Recognition

A frequent criticism of Indian popular cinema is that it isn't realistic. Critics point out technical shortcomings (a lot less these days), overstated performance and, of course, impossible songs within implausible stories as the examples of its lack of realism. On the other hand, popular cinema is also criticized for being escapist. But, as Sara Dickey (1993) shows in her study of poor urban viewers of Tamil cinema, popular films are expected by them to be a certain way. They certainly like to see wealth, luxury and all the other good things of consumer life even if that is unrepresentative of their own class condition. Like the gods, the stars too are expected to be ornamented in a fashion that reflects the high status they have in the hearts of their devotees. Along with wealth and pomp, Indian films also favour that other bugbear of film critics—a happy ending. A happy ending, however improbable, does not make it any less real for its audiences.

Unlike the more critically acclaimed realism of the great directors like Satyajit Ray, the realism of popular Indian cinema has been involved more with an emotional and moral concern rather than anything else. As Chakravarty writes:

The truth that the cinema was expected to 'capture' on the screen was not only the truth of social and psychological experience but the 'truth' of the right solution to moral dilemmas. (p. 99)

For a film culture that seems to ignore realism in terms of form, narrative and ideology, Indian cinema clearly takes the idea of 'truth' quite seriously. The popular theme of recognition suggests that the plot in such films hinges essentially on leaning away from the truth, and then, when we cannot stand it any more, coming right back to it in the happy ending. Long-lost brothers finding each other, the abandoned son finally winning his mother's love, the good daughter-in-law being vindicated and the mendacious one chastened are all examples of how recognition—of each other, and of the truth about each other—is central to popular cinema. The notion of multiple truths and leaving things hanging, or unrecognized, does not fit in well here. We do not have too many Rashomons, which might make us think about such matters. There is a truth, and if it is recognized, all's well that ends well, as they say.

Why is recognition important in Indian cinema? It may be possible to address this question again in terms of the negotiation between the modern and the non-modern, or to be precise, between the world of anonymity and that of familiarity. Indian notions of self, according to T.G. Vaidyanathan (1989), are largely relational. For example, when we ask, 'Who are you?' we expect to hear an answer in terms of someone's son, brother, cousin or even friend, rather than merely on the basis of the person's name or his job. That is perhaps inevitable in non-modern or partially modernized social contexts. In more modern social contexts, such as in the West, anonymity and a proclivity for individual identity would point the answer towards what one does, rather than whose relative one is. In the films of the 1970s, we see, in the process of urbanization, the breakdown in the old familiarity of the village. The protagonists are placed in an in-between modernity, where their older relationships to each other and to the land are no longer sustainable, but at the same time the new individual, agential self is not in any world that can sustain him either. Mobility is often seen in these films as the preserve of the immoral person, such as the smuggler. Although a small allowance is made for a morally sanctioned mobility as well, in this case the character would not be as wealthy, for example, as an upright police officer. However, in both the instances of the smuggler and the police officer, the characters' identities are anchored not in what they do, or even how they do it, but in who they are in relation to each other. By the end of the film, the truth about who they are and what they are to each other has to be sorted out and recognized as such.

Recognition is an important theme not only in cinema, but in Indian public culture as well. We may see it, as Varma (2004) suggests, as merely the ritual habit of a status-obsessed society, where everyone's interaction is deeply governed by the rules of hierarchy and deference. We can see it in politics, when communities organize themselves into voting blocs and demand shares of the pie. In the more recent globalization years, we can see how recognition (for India) has become an international priority, whether through speaking the language of nuclear tests, or in terms of seeking permanent representation on the UN Security Council. However, the theme of recognition in cinema, I think, suggests anything but a feudal obsession with status; nor identity politics of the sort that have dominated India since the 1980s. In cinema, it works to the contrary.

In the films, recognition is often preceded by misrecognition. The intensity with which mothers lose their memories, sight or children and then regain them at the end of a crushing and twisted saga of love and loss is perhaps a way of suggesting that modernity's heartless categories of knowledge (which are of course the stuff of the real world) result only in untruth, at least in the ideal world of the cinema. But in the end, when the truth is recognized, in terms of emotions, ethics, relationships and so on, we return to a non-modern assurance about the morality of the world and ourselves. It is in this manner perhaps that Indian cinema has either managed to sidestep or transcend the many uncanny trappings that arise when facing an audience that may be 'massified' at some superficial level, but is in actuality deeply and culturally divided. It is a remarkable achievement of democracy—but also of its popular cinema—that a small, centralized source of cultural production has achieved a measure of popular resonance across the divides of culture, taste and class. In a sense, if Gandhi discovered Indian universalism as a political practice and Nehru sought to give it a more Western and modern legal form, the films of India made its spirit live for its audiences, even when the differences, whether of class or of community, were deep, and perhaps insurmountable.

It is in this sense that we can appreciate how cinema has acquired a popular national form in India. The dominance of Hindi cinema over regional cinemas notwithstanding, we can appreciate how even local visions have been connected with a national one. The films in the regional languages, as we see in the following sections—even in the times of regionalism and strong anti-Hindi feelings in South India—did not abandon a stake in the nation. At the same time, as any sensitive or cynical critic can easily note, Indian films are full of stereotypes and politically incorrect caricatures. Even in the lofty days of Raj Kapoor, we see the stereotypes through which Bombay saw 'people from South' and Sikhs and Anglo-Indians, among others. But the social identities of characters in these films were always subsumed under who they were in their relationships, as this was ultimately more important to who they were as human beings. It was in this sense that their characters, or their true worth, would emerge, and not in the trappings of difference which made them Hindu, Muslim or Christian (or Amar, Akbar and Anthony for that matter).

In a later period, when identity politics of a sort did indeed become a reality in India, it became inevitable that these narrative endeavours towards a pan-Indian universalism had to address the categories in which these politics were playing out. It wasn't simply about the wronged brother being recognized as a good guy any more; it became about identities too. The Muslim had to be recognized as a fellow Indian. The militant had to recognize himself as a human being, a son, and come back from the jihadi brink. But the pleasure of recognition that Indian cinema gives us inevitably goes deeper into our hearts and our histories. We return to a humanistic universalism, of the sort that makes us recognize that everyone—the misunderstood hero, the misguided militant, the accused daughter—shares certain things as relational subjects, at the very least. This is what a diverse audience can always invest in, since it is indeed the most universal category, perhaps—they share the fact that they have all had mothers.

Indian popular cinema, in some ways, leaves reality to modernity, or equally, the other way around. Realism is thus less about a physical or rational representation, and more about a relational, emotional and ethical one. Even if the characters, sets, plots and everything else is unrealistic to the point of seeming like what Western viewers may call 'campy', the important thing in the Indian popular cinema is what we feel, and where we end up as a result of that feeling. When we watch, we are invited to recognize ourselves in our films as ethical subjects, and that recognition takes place not in a dry, rational manner but through emotional immersion in the travails and triumphs of the characters. It is an older form of seeking something called the 'truth', and it is perhaps far more universal than the belaboured, enumerated and politicized pursuits of universalism we find in modernity. It is not the literal or formal representation of communities, cities or ideologies that makes Indian cinema real. It becomes real when it makes you cry.

3

HOME

Doordarshan
Ramayan
NTR

IF 'COUNTRY' HAD BEEN THE REIGNING PREDILECTION OF INDIAN politics and cinema from the dawn of Independence, in the 1980s a new issue and a new medium came to dominate politics and popular culture. One way to characterize this transformation would be to see it as the beginning of a divergence between 'country' and 'home'. In some ways, the limitations of the sense of nation that had guided India in the Nehru era came to the fore, as regionalism became an important political force. Various groups of people in India began to politically assert demands rooted in different senses of home than the country had previously offered them. These were rooted, in one case, in linguistic identity, and in others in religious identity. In many cases, the role of media in general—and cinema, directly or indirectly—was very much in evidence in some of these developments. A legendary film star from a regional film industry led a call for the restoration of regional pride with profound political consequences on a national scale. A TV series turned the old tales of the gods into narratives that matched uncannily with new political assertions. In addition to these dramatic political and cultural expressions, there was a more mundane sense in which 'home' became a ruling theme of life in the 1980s—a new medium came home, literally, and brought with it dreams of the new sort of domesticity that a newly ascendant group in India was starting to experience as well—the middle class.

In this chapter, I consider three different ways in which

themes of home played out to form the way India began to
see itself during the 1980s. The first of these has to do with
the rise of television. Although TV broadcasting had existed
in India since the Nehru era, it was only in the 1980s that TV
became a truly widespread medium. It was also around this
time that TV became commercialized, marking the beginning
of what at the time was a new concern for the medium—the
lives of the urban middle classes as seen in sitcoms and soaps
(and advertisements). The second issue I discuss in this
chapter is the political career of the Telugu film-god N.T.
Rama Rao and the way in which a cinematic image and a real-
life political moment coincided. I show how NTR's political
triumphs were not merely the result of a generic star appeal,
but drew on his stature and his symbolism as someone who
would represent the poor and the marginalized. The third
issue I cover in this chapter is the phenomenally popular epic
series *Ramayan* and how its storytelling rendered it from the
realm of the mythic or the devotional imagination into a
historic one as well, coinciding with the rise of a new political
perception of India as a Hindu homeland. I also situate these
three themes in the light of their political and economic roots
during the Nehru era, and suggest how these developments
may have paved the way for the sort of media climate that
came to be in the following decade.

The Political and Economic Roots of Home

The seeds for the sort of political and cultural demands for
regional aspirations and domestic comforts that came to the
fore in the 1980s were sown much earlier. Although the birth
of independent India is frequently seen in relation to the
horrors of Partition, the Hindu–Muslim question was not

the only one that the newly independent nation had to deal with. In some ways, regional and linguistic identities have always remained more salient everyday markers of peoples' sense of themselves than religious identity alone. Thus, even if Partition was a traumatic event for Hindus and Muslims from certain regions of India like Punjab and Bengal, other regional aspirations also played a role in how India came to be.

One of the most important steps that took place in the formation of independent India was the linguistic organization of states. As Guha (2007) writes, '(f)or Kannadigas and Andhras, for Oriyas and Maharashtrians, language proved a more powerful marker of identity than caste or religion' (p. 207). Shortly after Independence, Telugu-speaking people living in the Madras province demanded their own state. Their leader, Potti Sriramulu, fasted for fifty-eight days to support this demand and lost his life in the process. Nehru gave in to the demand for a separate state and, in 1956, Andhra Pradesh was born. Soon, other states too began to be reorganized on a linguistic basis, leading Guha to comment that if Nehru was the 'maker of modern India', then Sriramulu was perhaps its 'Mercator'. Despite the fears of balkanization that this process raised, Guha writes, 'linguistic reorganization seems rather to have consolidated the unity of India' (p. 208).

The matter of national language, of course, did evoke powerful resistance in South India and especially in Tamil Nadu, where a strong anti-Hindi political sentiment existed. Although Gandhi had been a sincere believer in replacing English—the language left behind by the colonial elite—with Hindi as the official national language, the attempt to turn this into policy infuriated the South. Hindi was wisely enough not sought to be 'imposed' any more, and the informal notion of the 'three language' formula ((English, Hindi and a regional language) came to stay across much of India where Hindi was not spoken locally. Although the rise of regionalism in the 1980s was not a demand for the preservation of linguistic identity in the same manner as the earlier opposition to Hindi, it did arise at the moment when unrecognized local aspirations found a voice in the rise of newly prosperous and politically assertive local communities.

The second source of the rise of regionalism, religious nationalism and middle-class aspirations in the 1980s lay in the consequences of the economic vision that India followed soon after Independence. Had Gandhi had his way, this would not have been the path India followed at all. Instead of pursuing the ideals of social and economic modernization which Nehru embodied, India would have perhaps returned to a loose federation of self-sustaining village republics guided by a small elite following the lofty principles of 'trusteeship'. However, becoming a nation of high thinking and simple living, as the saying goes, was already past the realm of possibility by the time of Independence. The exceptions of the great men and women of that generation notwithstanding, the first rulers of independent India did not differ too much from the British in their understanding of the nation and what was good for it. As Khilnani (1999) writes:

> [T]he Congress party ... had arrived at independence uncommitted to any decisive economic strategy. There was

broad agreement about the problems that faced free India
[such as] poverty [but] . . . [t]he proposed solutions varied.
(p. 64)

The solution that would prevail was a Nehruvian vision of
modernization. India, as Khilnani puts it evocatively, fell in
love with concrete and statistics. Dams became the new
temples, and economic planners were the new sages. India
was thinking of itself on a scale of modernization that was not
quite what Gandhi would have wanted. With centralized
planning, and in time, the Green Revolution, the result would
be economic growth, the concern about its 'Hindu rate'
notwithstanding. In three decades, the Green Revolution
would yield its bounties, and its social and political side
effects too. It would increase production, but also sow the
seeds for the rise of a middle peasant class that would make
demands that could no longer be met within the old elite-
mass framework of the Congress party.

The economic policies of the Nehru and Indira Gandhi
periods thus sowed the seeds of at least one important political
group which would rise and bring into focus its own particular
notions of national culture. If Nehru himself was an English-
educated liberal modernizer, the elites of the 1980s would
come to include both a somewhat Westernized urban middle
class, and a large number of non-Westernized middle classes,
whose culture I describe later in this chapter as one of
'vernacular modernity'. The world of TV, and in one state,
cinema, would revolve around these new groups and their
aspirations throughout the 1980s.

Home Comforts: The Rise of Doordarshan

As Rachel Dwyer and Divia Patel (2002) point out, the staircase was the reigning symbol of privileged domesticity in Indian cinema. In innumerable films about patriarchs, landlords, joint families, domestic intrigues and even romances, the grand stairway dominates the set. Usually, the shot opens by revealing a large hall, with the staircase rising up at its back. There are variations on the staircase itself. Sometimes, there is one single flight of stairs going all the way up. Sometimes, there is a landing halfway and the stairs split up into two opposite directions. The landing is sometimes accentuated with chandeliers, or with stuffed animal heads. Many scenes have played out on these steps. It makes for a grand entrance for characters like wealthy zamindars who may be corrupt, or, as in some of the noblesse oblige films of the Nehru era, just kindly patriarchs who walk down grandly as estate managers and loyal orderlies await reverentially downstairs. In the Angry Young Man era, the vile father of the heroine could use the stairs to make a point about his class superiority over the hero. In the definitive family film of the 1990s, *Hum Aapke Hain Koun..!*, one of the characters suddenly trips over the steps of such a sweeping stairway to an untimely demise.

The staircase and the grand hall remain a pervasive theme in Indian cinema (and in some of the more recent TV soap operas about scheming families too), but in the 1980s, a new image of home began to form, in real life and in the TV programmes that came to celebrate it. The sort of idealized home that was the location of the stories of the decade was neither the heavens of the mythologicals, nor the zamindar's mansion, nor the slum of the angry young man films—it was simply a middle-class flat, often in a 'complex'. It was small and full of people—families, neighbours, orderlies, visitors. It had all the gadgets that middle-class India was beginning to purchase in large numbers. There was a gas stove, a fridge and, most of all, perhaps to compensate for the loss of that grand staircase, a TV set. It was the beginning of the age of middle-class domesticity in India, and it was on TV as much as TV was a part of it.

Although TV had been available in India for many years, it was only in the early 1980s that it turned into a widespread phenomenon, and a commercial, urban-middle-class-oriented one at that. When broadcasting began in the late 1950s, it was envisioned very much as a development tool, rather than as an entertainment or commercial medium. As Anjali Monteiro (1998) writes, 'Television was . . . expected to break down traditional values, disseminate technical skills, foster national integration and accelerate the growth of formal education' (p. 158). The mandate for Doordarshan was thus derived from what she aptly calls the 'messianic' language of development. Before the 1980s, the programmes were mostly aimed at rural audiences, and included educational features and adult literacy classes. In the bigger cities, there was the occasional *Lucy Show*, but on the whole, programming used to be largely Indian-made and educational. Hyderabad Doordarshan, for example, is perhaps most remembered from the 1970s for *Paalu Chelu*, a how-to programme for farmers that often annoyed the urban middle class with its monotonous footage about the proper methods to care for one's cows and crops. The most popular programming during that period, though, was unsurprisingly film-based. The weekend films and the weekly film-song shows, like *Chitrahaar*, were the main form of whatever entertainment Doordarshan had to offer.

Even the process of remembering TV before the 1980s from the standpoint of the present seems strange because of the relative lack of importance of the consumer in its scheme of things. TV had come about from a different social vision, and its place in it was seen as largely instrumental. Nehru had thought of it as a tool to change the 'traditional' attitudes of Indians and help them modernize through the adoption of rational and scientific attitudes. However, Doordarshan also came to be seen perhaps as nothing more than a tool for propagating the virtues of the ruling party and its leaders. Even the first move to change the direction of TV through commercialization and expansion of broadcasting in the early 1980s had at least a few expectations of political and propaganda benefits.

Indira Gandhi and the Congress party had returned to power in the elections of 1980, and were dealing with the new constituencies that had acquired enough power to make demands of the state and the party by this time. Among these were the middle classes and the push towards a consumer-driven economy. In the emerging world view, TV was seen, both by the leaders and the middle classes, not merely as a tool for modernization but as a symbol of a new kind of modernity in itself—a consumer one, and a nationalist one too. In 1982, India—it may be said in the spirit of the athletes in whose name it happened—made a great leap forward in TV and in real life. It hosted an international sporting event in New Delhi on a spectacular scale—the Asian Games. Purnima Mankekar (1999) writes: 'The Asiad provided the state with opportunity to convey its image as a modern nation capable of hosting and organizing an international sports event, not just to the rest of the world, but to its own citizens' (p. 56).

The live coverage of the opening of the Asian Games was virtually unprecedented in its reach. In the months preceding the Games and after, large numbers of TV 'kendras' (centres) and transmitters were set up and a nationally broadcast 'National Programme' became a regular occurrence as well. For the first time, India had a national TV audience, and its first feast of sorts was the Asian Games. The Games evoked a sense of national accomplishment. The image of Appu the dancing elephant mascot was ubiquitous and made its way across the drawing boards of children's art contests and on to the covers of their notebooks. In a country almost singularly devoted to the worship of cricket, people did indeed take an interest in the other sports that were played at the Asiad. Every day, there were discussions about how many medals India had won, and how it stood in relation to the big achievers like China. In any case, the biggest achievement for India was not in any one contest, but in perhaps putting on the show itself; and putting it into millions of homes, and in colour at that. Although the coverage of the Games did not directly glorify the ruling party or its leaders (the news was rather more single-mindedly dedicated to that), their attendance at the events was frequently noted by the cameras and, in the rising middle-class optimism of the time, seemed quite in order really.

With a show and a TV set, the Indian middle class's entry into TV and modernity began in full earnest. The government had not merely set up its transmitting infrastructure, but had also ensured that TV could be more affordable than it had been in the past. By cutting import duties and encouraging domestic production, it initiated a consumer revolution. The number of TV sets sold in India increased from 2.8 million in

1983 to 11 million in 1988 (Mankekar, 1999). It was obviously
not merely the possessive drive for TV sets that drove this
increase (although one of the most famous ads for a TV
brand infamously labelled it 'neighbour's envy, owner's
pride'), but what was on it. In 1983, Doordarshan began to
invite commercial sponsorships of programmes and, for the
first time, the state-owned network entered into the business
of making money as well. With a massive middle-class
audience available for advertisers to push the products that
were now being sold widely, sponsored entertainment
programmes and some very entertaining advertisements
began to proliferate on television.

As a state-run institution, Doordarshan's commercialization
took place with some paternalistic caution, as was to be
expected. As Mankekar writes, there were fears that
commercialization would lead to unbridled consumerism
and 'foreign' influences, and the early serials were well rooted
in the idea and ideals of development. Doordarshan, it was
believed by its directors, needed to have an 'Indian personality'
and not abjure its development goals either. It was with such
a combination of the ideals of national development and
entertainment that some of the first fictional series were
produced. The first TV series in India to enjoy phenomenal
popularity was *Hum Log* (beginning 1984), which Mankekar
describes as the 'story of a lower middle class family struggling
to achieve upward mobility and become middle class'
(p. 70). Following the lead of a Peruvian telenovela, *Hum Log*
sought to combine 'social messages' with entertainment.
Mankekar notes that *Hum Log* was quite a hybrid, with Indian-
cinema-style melodrama and an American-soap-opera-style
structure. It was like an Indian film to the extent that it was

about family relationships and played out in the familiar language of emotions, but it was also different as a media experience in that its reception was domestic and seemingly unending. As India's first soap opera, *Hum Log* led to the usual commentary, critique and witticisms, as the middle-class homes of India suddenly discovered a new loyalty to their TV sets and the watching of *Hum Log* became a regular ritual across the country. Since it was not yet a time when every household or even most household had TV sets, despite its rapid proliferation, it was still quite common to see large groups of neighbours and children gather in the homes of those who did.

In the years that followed, a number of entertainment programmes captured the nation's fancy. Mankekar writes that by 1987, forty serials had been indigenously produced and telecast on Doordarshan. These included *Buniyaad* (beginning 1986), a dramatic story about a family displaced by Partition, and *Tamas* (1986), a critically acclaimed mini-series also about the violence of Partition. As the serials grew, so did their scope. It was no longer just middle-class apartments that appeared on these shows. *Khandaan* (beginning 1985), a soap opera set in the lives of wealthy business families, raised the class bar by turning to a setting of glamour and luxury, a far cry from the rural imagery on the TV of the earlier era. Wealthy urban youth were the subject of another serial with presumably the same sort of mandate to combine commercially viable entertainment with a pro-social message. *Subah* (beginning 1987) sought to depict the evils of drug abuse by featuring an attractive set of fashionable college students who turn on and trip out to images and sounds vaguely evocative of the psychedelic era.

The moral of *Subah* was regrettably lost when the serial was terminated before the audience could see the characters get their comeuppance. While we do not know whether it achieved its goal of fighting drug abuse (or the contrary), one fashion trend seen on this series did proliferate in college campuses at this time—that of tail shirts over jeans and slippers.

Middle-class domesticity was also the subject of a number of sitcoms which mirrored the breezy, happy, urban middle-class lifestyle that was spreading in India. *Yeh Jo Hai Zindagi* (beginning 1984) featured a set of recognizable characters that people in any 'colony' or 'complex' across India could relate to. While the protagonists in the soap consisted of a young couple and a single brother, there were often other characters who added to the fun, including one actor whose appearance in a variety of roles was a much-awaited part of the experience. Even the title sequence of the soap celebrated urban pleasures and quotidian delights, like an evening out at the beach or simply waiting for the bus. Increasingly, the sets and décor of the apartments or homes in which these fictional characters lived seemed to mirror those of a new visual discourse that was growing on TV—that of advertising.

Before Doordarshan's commercialization, the only advertising that was watched in India was the handful of commercials that often flanked documentaries made by the Films Division of India and shown at the theatre before the main feature. Throughout the 1980s, TV advertising (and advertising in general) grew in quantity and imagination. Some of the characters and their punchlines became iconic, such as the character Lalitaji, a smart, no-nonsense homemaker who snaps at the male voice-over to declare that there is no harm in spending a little more for something good. There were signature tunes, such as the jingle that rang out from TV and radio sets to announce the arrival of a washing powder which promised to make clothes whiter than milk. There were also advertisements that played on anxiety and offence, albeit in a slightly softer manner than those of early-twentieth-century American advertising perhaps. In an instance quite symbolic of how TV, modernity and consumerism had all spread throughout not only the geographical space of the nation but also into the private space of the family, a popular ad starts with a salesman asking a prospective customer how much he loves his wife. 'What is your meaning?' the offended customer asks, rather strongly. The salesman, still smiling, explains. If the man loves his wife a lot, then only the brand of pressure cooker that is being advertised is right for him. Money may not have bought love, but it was now being increasingly seen as buying the image of love.

TV had come home in more ways than one. It was bringing with it demands for the reconfiguration not merely of the drawing room furniture and daily schedules of work, homework and play, but also of how people related to one another. When children were hungry, TV knew what mommy had to do. She would say, 'Two minutes!', and the famous instant-food package of the 1980s—the '2 Minute Noodles'— would be prepared instantly. The noodle makers paid for the production costs of *Hum Log*, and in turn sold massive quantities of the ubiquitous coloured packages. In retrospect, the used wrappers that would float around the roads and waste dumps also marked the beginning of another feature of an emerging environment, the proliferation of plastic and packaging waste that would not disappear. On the other hand, though, it was a tasty snack, and it was quick and convenient, like the new rhythms of work and life that were starting to emerge. Although the rise of the Indian middle class and its new urban habitat of apartment complexes did not quite parallel the latchkey phenomenon of the American suburb around the same time, it was the start also of a process of fragmentation. The era of the extended family, and that of the independent house too, was over. The traditional marriage, too, was facing its challenges. As Mankekar notes, there were numerous cases of dowry demands that the participants of her study attributed to consumerism and TV. If TV was transforming ideas of tradition, there were also wider signs of acknowledgement in the media of other kinds of relationships. One well-known Hindi film of the early 1980s, *Masoom* (1983), showed the story of a child born out of a man's relationship before marriage. Made by Shekhar Kapur, *Masoom* indeed captured a sense of innocence, set in contrast to the upper-class cosmopolitan urban life, and also managed to suggest a way of living one's relationships ethically that did not have to be a screaming saga for mother and for an unchanging notion of 'family values'.

Home Pride: NTR

There was certainly a pan-Indianness to the ideal and experience of urban middle-class domesticity during the 1980s, especially in the context of TV. To a certain extent, that sort of Indianness carried with it its own form of cosmopolitanism, borne perhaps out of an old Nehruvian sense of education and Westernization. In elite schools, for example, it was unlikely one even knew what one's 'caste' was. In the complexes, or especially in the 'colonies' that had accompanied the vast public-sector undertakings of the Nehru era, a sort of middle-class unity in diversity existed. It was the peculiarity of a time that lay between the familiar ties of the village and the extreme anonymity of the megacities of the 1990s. The middle-class Indianness of the 1980s was just about being Indian in a broad, national sense.

However, the rise of a pan-Indian middle class was only one part of the forces that came to the fore during the 1980s. This was also the time that saw the rise of groups whose ascendancy did not express itself in national terms, but in quite the opposite: in regionalism. In Punjab, Kashmir, the North East and in South India, the rise of new groups and aspirations began to change Indian politics and, in at least one state, that change was deeply rooted in its films. Unlike the deadly form regionalism took in other parts of India, in Andhra Pradesh, regionalism surged into politics in the idiom of drama and emotion, not in the least because its face was the Telugu film industry's greatest star, the legendary N.T. Rama Rao. His transformation from a mythological film star to a political leader took place on the strength of a charisma of such magnitude that nearly twenty years later, Shashi Tharoor (15 August 2003) would write, 'Arnold Schwarzenegger . . . may become governor of California, but he can't become God (like NTR).'

NTR's popularity and his subsequent political career may be best appreciated in the context of the history and politics of South Indian cinema in general. As Dickey (1996) writes, 'more films are produced and watched per capita in South India than anywhere else in the world' (p. 131). South India has also had the distinction of perhaps having more film stars in politics than any other part of the world. Even before NTR's entry into politics, his Tamil counterpart, M.G. Ramachandran (MGR), had been elected Chief Minister of Tamil Nadu. Following the rise of NTR, numerous other film stars also become active in politics and by the end of the decade, many national and regional film stars would have served in state or national politics.

It is sometimes easy to attribute the political success of film stars to a generic notion of charisma (as indeed the presence of Ronald Reagan in the White House at the same time might imply). In the case of some of the film stars who reigned in South Indian politics though, it was a more complex set of factors than their mere 'crowd-pulling' talents that was at stake. These factors included political realignments among newly ascendant communities and the broad mass appeal that the stars had on the strength of not only who they were, but also on the sort of roles they had played. NTR's image drew on a whole range of heroic roles that he had played over the decades. From his mythological classics, he was Krishna. From his more recent action films, he was the noble but no-nonsense tough guy. In any form, though, his image spoke to the masses, especially to the poor.

NTR made his film debut in the late 1940s. Telugu cinema had been in existence for close to two decades now, and its most notable films were either the mythologicals and the saint films, or social films with sometimes progressive messages about women's rights and other issues. Although there were numerous actors who had acquired a great deal of respect for their work, Telugu cinema did not necessarily have a star until this time. It was only in 1951, in the folklore/

fantasy hit *Patala Bhairavi* (1951) that the notion of the hero as a star was explicitly presented. As S.V. Srinivas (2001) observes, the narrative of this film was unique for the time in casting the protagonist as a heroic figure, and the film established certain conventions for the deification of the male lead that continued into numerous social genres as well. Throughout the 1950s and '60s, NTR remained one of the major stars of Telugu cinema, appearing as Lord Krishna in numerous mythologicals, including the ever-popular *Maya Bazar*, as well as Ravana in the 1956 film *Bhukailasa*. Then, when changes in financing and general industry culture in the 1970s led to the rise of colour action films, paralleling the rise of the Angry Young Man genre in Hindi cinema, NTR's roles changed accordingly. From the late 1970s, he starred in a series of films with the suffix 'Ramudu' and another with the suffix '-gadu' (dude). The titles included hits like *Adavi Ramudu* (1977), *Vetagadu* (1979) and *Circus Ramudu* (1980). These films combined the lost-at-birth stories of the time with intrigue, villainy and action, and featured a somewhat less youthful-looking NTR now dancing with a set of young leading ladies in songs with bawdy lyrics. NTR also made a Telugu *Superman* (1980) and essayed a character with a similar cape and suit, albeit with a different source of superpower (the god Hanuman). In an interesting return to mythology (which would take place again later in the 1980s), NTR also wrote, directed and starred in three major roles in a 1977 production called *Dana Veera Shura Karna*. The film focused on Karna, the first of the Pandava brothers, who is abandoned at birth and ends up fighting on the side of the Kauravas against his own brothers. In this film, one can see the Angry Young Man sensibility of the noble hero abandoned by the mother, as well as a populist questioning of injustices done against certain characters in the story. *Dana Veera Shura Karna* was not quite an oppositional reading of the sacred epic, but it certainly capitalized on elements of it that expressed a sense of abandonment and injustice.

When NTR entered politics in 1982, though, he was greeted not as Superman or even as Krishna (although he was worshipped on par with him, presumably), but simply as 'anna' or elder brother (J. Neuss, 1998). What he represented to his supporters was not literally either a god or a superhero, but the possibility perhaps of justice in the real world, much as he had delivered it in many of his films. For the poor, NTR was indeed a saviour, someone who had defeated the rich, the evil and the greedy in his films, and could perhaps do the same in politics as well. As Dickey (1996) observes in her study of poor Tamil cinema viewers, the sort of 'utopia' that the films of the time offered the poor was interpreted not merely as an 'escape', but as a source of hope for the recognition of the morality of the poor, and perhaps their entitlement to better material conditions as well. At the same time, it was not only the poor who were responsible for NTR's electoral success. As K. Balagopal (1995) writes:

> The birth of the Telugu Desam party . . . was the political consequence of at least two phenomena. One is the dissatisfaction felt by a certain section of Andhra's regional elite with the Congress party . . . Those sections of the regional landed-financial-commercial elite . . . such as the rich among the Kammas of coastal Andhra Pradesh—felt that they deserved more political power. (p. 2482)

NTR thus represented not only the dreams of the poor, but also the interests of a politically and economically ascendant community. NTR's campaign was strongly supported by a privileged social base and by its own investment in the media; his political fortunes grew alongside those of a new regional newspaper called *Eenadu*, which by the 1990s would grow into one of the largest media groups in India (R. Jeffrey, 1997). The rise of all these forces may have constituted in some ways what may be thought of as 'vernacular modernities' in India. If the Nehru era had laid in place one form of modernity that one may associate with the English-educated pan-Indian middle classes, by the 1980s the rise of elites and middle classes in regional language groups was also in evidence. Unlike the relatively more Westernized urban middle classes, vernacular moderns inhabited a cultural world rooted in local-language media, be it cinema or news. They only embraced the aspects of modernity that they desired, such as an investment in medicine and technology, laying the foundations perhaps for the rise of Andhra Pradesh as an important Information Technology hub in the following decade. In any case, regional identity, and a sense of pride about it, would emerge as an important political factor for them, even as NTR would become the most visible symbol of it.

Given that Telugu cinema seldom expressed regional rage or perhaps even aspiration, it is thus doubly interesting that NTR would ride into prominence on the singular issue of 'Telugu self-respect'. Unlike some other regions, Andhra Pradesh did not have a history of separatist sentiment. The Indian national flag, it is often proudly noted, was designed by a Telugu patriot. The Telugu people of the Telangana region were instrumental in forcing the integration of the erstwhile princely state of Hyderabad into the Indian union

after Independence, despite violent opposition from local
Muslim extremists. Even at the time of the language riots in
South India during the 1960s, Andhra Pradesh did not quite
lose its sense of itself as a part of India. It was politically a
staunch Congress state, where, despite the communist
strongholds, the charisma of 'Amma' (or mother, as Indira
Gandhi was called) was enough to win elections unfailingly
for the party. In 1977, when much of India rejected the
Congress, Andhra Pradesh still voted for its Amma. When
she lost the election in her own home state of Uttar Pradesh,
it was to Medak in Andhra Pradesh that Mrs Gandhi would
come to seek re-election. But all of this history would fall in
one swift move in a moment that belonged to NTR and the
newfound sense of regional pride he embodied.

By the early 1980s, the once-unchallenged support for the
Congress party was disturbed increasingly by a growing
popular resentment at what in those days was called the
'remote control rule' by New Delhi. The Congress leadership
in the state was seen as lacking in integrity and subservient to
the whims of the national leadership. Even though the
Congress won the elections, it could not, it seems, stay
happy—four different Chief Ministers would come and go in
a very short span (the blame for which, to be fair, should not
be put on New Delhi alone but on the local factions as well).
One such Chief Minister, the affable T. Anjaiah, found himself
in a fiasco which would effectively hand NTR his platform. In
an effusive show of Hyderabadi hospitality that lent itself
easily to charges of sycophancy, Anjaiah's government had
organized a grand welcome at the airport for the arrival of
Rajiv Gandhi, who had only recently joined politics. When
Anjaiah and his colleagues rushed to the plane to garland

him, Rajiv Gandhi reportedly lost his temper and berated the Chief Minister in public. The newspapers carried the pictures the next morning; all of Andhra Pradesh saw its chastised Chief Minister and a seemingly imperious Prime Minister's heir apparent. As Guha (2007) writes about this incident, 'the humiliation was felt personally and collectively, with the Telugu media portraying it as insult to the pride of the Andhras' (p. 549).

One month later, NTR launched the Telugu Desam Party (TDP) and began to tour the state on an improvised 'chariot'. As Guha writes, 'he was the mythological hero made real, come to rid the world of greed and corruption and bring justice for all' (p. 549). The impact of NTR's campaigning was massive. It was strongly layered with mythological themes—giant cut-outs of him as Krishna, blowing the conch to sound the start of the war, rose up everywhere. In his party posters, he stood dramatically with his finger pointing upward, exhorting the people. Cassettes with his bombastic speeches circulated widely (he was a formidable orator). The people honoured him when he went to their villages as if he were indeed an avatar. They broke coconuts and washed his feet with the water. They offered him aartis. They made very sure that his party won, and without an ounce of prevarication at that. In January 1983, the TDP won by a massive margin and NTR took his oath of office in a spectacular public gathering in Hyderabad's premier cricket stadium. Although this victory for Telugu pride should have remained in its home state, in just about a year, a political misadventure orchestrated by the Congress party would end up making NTR a national hero.

In August 1984, when NTR was in the US for heart surgery,

a group of dissidents attempted to overthrow his government with political support from the Congress. For one month, an interim Chief Minister attempted to prove his strength in the house, as NTR loyalists among the representatives hide themselves away (or were hidden, as the story goes) first in his studios, where they watched his old films for inspiration, and then at a resort in neighbouring Karnataka. Finally, they were taken to New Delhi, where a dramatic photo on the steps of Rashtrapati Bhavan showed the nation that he had the numbers, and that democracy was under threat in India. One month later, as Hyderabad burnt under what in those days were the fairly frequent communal riots (between Hindus and Muslims), and Doordarshan vainly broadcast special afternoon films in a bid to keep people off the streets, NTR returned to power. His return was such a matter of pride to his people that even the assassination of Indira Gandhi a few months later, and the massive sympathy vote this gave the Congress across the country, could not deter his victory at the polls. In December 1984, when the country witnessed the fearful spectacle of a slick ad campaign that asked ominous questions about the future of India in an age beset by terrorism, the people of Andhra Pradesh ignored all such caution and quietly voted for NTR all over again.

In his years as Chief Minister, NTR presided over some attempts to bring his Telugu pride mandate into policy. One of his legacies was a row of statues of important historical figures on the promenade of the Tank Bund, a large lake in the centre of Hyderabad. The statues included emperors like Krishna Deva Raya of the Vijayanagara empire, and great poets and singers like Vemana and Tyagaraja. The most ambitious of these monuments, though, was a gigantic rock-carved Buddha, which was set up on an island in the middle of the lake (after one attempt fatally failed). The rumour, of course, was that the latter was done to coincide with a film NTR made about the Buddha, and that the former was a megalomaniacal indulgence on an unbelievably cinematic scale—all the faces of the great Telugu people on the statues of the Tank Bund seem to resemble NTR, as if he were playing them in his films. His alleged eccentricities entertained the urban middle classes, especially when he announced he had renounced the world and started to wear ascetic's clothes, at a time when rumours also circulated of how corrupt his government was. He attempted a comeback film, and was photographed attending to official papers in full costume at the studio. By the late 1980s, despite his one truly populist policy of cheap rice for the poor, NTR's charisma could not hold the state. The Congress party found a way to hit back by recruiting a number of other film stars. An anti-NTR satire film was also made at this time. NTR meanwhile had captured the growing opposition to the Congress on a nationwide scale, and helped forge a united opposition party. Guha quotes his memorable lines on the occasion, as NTR describes the new party as a chariot 'drawn by seven horses [that] will dispel the gloom and shadows that thickened through the passage of the last few decades of national history' (p. 590).

In the elections of 1989, every political and cultural tendency in India that had sparked and crackled during the decade made its mark on the election results. For the first time, India had a hung parliament. The Congress was indeed removed from power, but in the new coalition, which included Left, Right, caste-based and region-based parties, one important constituent was missing. NTR's Telugu Desam party lost most of its seats in the Parliamentary and Assembly elections. The chariot's lead horse would not be there to take its place in history. Although he would never become Prime Minister, NTR's moment in the history of modern India cannot be discounted. A film god did change the course not only of the state of the people who adored him, but indeed, of the country too.

Homelands: *Ramayan*

Home pride, especially of the Telugu sort, was quite a modest affair in comparison to the bigger reimagining of nation and community that started to take place by the late 1980s. The new middle-class modernity was the basis not just for regional aspirations, but for a rising new political force with strong pan-Indian ambitions—the Hindutva movement. Hindutva was by no means an isolated resurgence, and took place in close proximity to both the regionalist politics and the casteist politics of the time. Its propaganda was quick and effective, and it was aided, if not abetted, by the wild popularity of two serials on Doordarshan that effectively (if not wholly, or even intentionally) turned the focus of the Ramayana and the Mahabharata from 'God' (as I explained in the first chapter) to 'religion' (as I explain below). The difference was not just a matter of faith, or of secularism, but of the politics of the time as well. Andhra Pradesh, after all, had a much longer and deeper engagement with a media tradition of mythologicals than the Hindi-speaking regions. NTR was widely identified with his mythological roles, especially Krishna; but the gods in his case were brought into politics only to the extent of standing for justice, rather than necessarily for advancing a 'Hindu' political agenda. However, in the wake of the nationally telecast religious epics, the same gods were now called upon to serve as symbols of a powerful and, at times, militant movement. Neither the cause of Telugus nor Hindus may have diminished the deeper significance of what Rama and Krishna may have meant to the devout, but the conflation between religion as practice and as politics came close in this period, and seemed almost identical in the eyes of many left-wing academics and critics.

One media phenomenon, the Sunday morning Doordarshan serial *Ramayan* (beginning 1987), was taken to task in particular for contributing to this state more than any other. Its fans, though, sang its praises, despite its many aesthetic and ideological shortcomings. For them, it was about revering 'Ram' (as he is called in the series), learning about good conduct and the like, which was no different perhaps from the old mythological films. But at the same time, it was also increasingly about learning about one's 'heritage', one's roots and about enjoying the solidarity of being part of an imagined community of Hindu-Indians, which was indeed somewhat different from the implication or consequence of the old mythologicals. Some important questions thus need to be asked. Why did being 'Hindu' somehow become more important than being a devotee of God? What was the history of thinking of one's self as Hindu or Muslim?

The modern notion of Hindus and Muslims (and of various castes too) had their origins in the tightly defined categories of the British administrators' instruments of rule, such as the census. This move marked a change in how communities saw themselves and others at this time—a change that Kaviraj (1992) characterizes as a shift from 'fuzzy' to 'enumerated' communities. Before this change, there were indeed Hindus and Muslims in India, but the difference was in how they saw themselves, and more importantly, how the state viewed them. The lines of identity drawn (or 'inscribed', as the textbooks would say) by colonial discourses across the lives of people had great political consequences, ranging from the creation of separate electorates by the British (the old 'divide and rule' precept) to the ultimate manifestation—the partition of India on religious lines. Despite the demands for a reciprocal Hindu state expressed in some quarters, post-Independence India stayed constitutionally secular. Nehru's secularism may have theoretically been closer to his liberal Western ideal, but in practice, it was perhaps closer to both the demands of coexistence in a modern nation and the more non-modern notions of tolerance embodied most nobly by Gandhi.

Even if religious identity, as Hindus and Muslims, became a reality under British colonialism, it did not mitigate the various ways in which tolerance was practised in daily life. As Suketu Mehta (2004) observes, there is not necessarily a great sense of affection between different communities in everyday Indian life, but a studied and balanced distance between one another based on a clear understanding of each other. He describes the views of a local 'hothead' from the Bombay slums: 'In the villages, you live very close to your neighbors and everybody knows everybody's business and their families and predilections. There is very little mobility; you will have to live together all your lives and can't afford blood feuds with your neighbors' (p. 64). If the practical demands of coexistence place limits on how much one can live as Hindus and Muslims in opposition to each other, there are other, internal limitations to the Hindu identity as well. The notion

of being Hindu in general is often less meaningful to a
Hindu than being a Hindu in a specific form—as one of
thousands of communities marked by region, language and
the notion broadly called caste. If one were to add a further
religious mandate to the definition, then being a Hindu is
also about being a part of one or more traditional or
modern spiritual traditions (the latter, of course, usually
being open to non-Hindus as well), of following a certain
guru, perhaps. However, in the 1980s, in the wake of a time
of complex and turbulent politics, the idea of a Hindu nation
rose into prominence as an 'imagined community', indeed
even as a more 'enumerated' way of thinking about being
Hindu also spread across the popular consciousness. The
reasons for this of course, go far beyond the Ramayana in
general or the TV *Ramayan* in particular. (I use the spellings
'Ramayan' for the Hindi TV series and 'Ramayana' for general
usage; similarly, 'Ram' for TV and political usage, 'Rama' for
general.)

'In the first years of independence,' Guha writes, 'the
wounds of partition had provided an excuse for a vigorous
assertion by the Hindu right. The RSS was particularly active.
But when the Jana Sangh won only three seats in the election
of 1952, commentators were ready to write an epitaph for a
party that, in a modern, secular, democratic state, dared to
base its politics on religion' (pp. 634–35). Throughout the
Nehru and Indira Gandhi eras, the political fortunes of the
Hindu nationalist parties rose slightly and fell, and at the
start of the fateful decade, in the elections of 1984, the BJP
won two seats out of 500 or so. Five years later, it would
emerge much stronger with eighty-six seats, and support the
non-Congress government of V.P. Singh as well, before

pulling out support to begin the intense mobilization with which it was to be identified—the 'Ram Janmabhoomi' movement. Its goal was to 'liberate' the site which was believed to be the birthplace of Lord Ram by demolishing a mosque believed to have been built by the invading Mughal emperor Babar centuries ago. The dispute over the site had its origins in the nineteenth century, when the belief that the mosque had been built over a demolished temple gained ground. Shortly after Independence, an idol of a child Lord Ram was placed in a makeshift shrine inside the mosque. The structure was eventually closed to both communities, and remained out of the public agenda until the mid-1980s, when a series of political moves led to its seemingly unwitting reawakening. The rise of regionalism in the 1980s was by no means unrelated to the rise of Hindu nationalism, although one should logically have weakened the other. NTR was famous for invoking his 'six crore (sixty million) Telugu people', and by the middle of the decade, another larger figure was being echoed across the political arena—the 'sixty crore (six hundred million) Hindu people' in whose name the Hindu nationalist forces were fighting (Guha, p. 639). Enumeration, in a sense, was becoming popular rhetoric, even as the centrality of 'vote banks' to the political game grew. As Khilnani writes, democracies involve more than a simple process of individuals rationally choosing their representatives, but require a 'larger cultural connection'. Political identities do not necessarily have a 'pre-political existence' but have to be 'created through politics' (p. 49).

These identities were, of course, not based merely on religion, but on many other distinctions—real, imagined or enumerated—including caste, class, tribe, religious nationalism and nativism. Against this complex picture, elections became increasingly a question of management and accommodation, and sometimes conflict over identities, and less about intellectual positions and debate. The Hindu nationalist organizations were always aware of the resentment that existed about the Congress party's supposed pandering to minorities (either over the question of the uniform civil code, or the more contentious issue of Kashmir, with its territorial and symbolic overlaps with the issues of Pakistan and terrorism as well). In 1986, they received a political gift unexpectedly. Rajiv Gandhi had started his term rich on the middle class's hopes for indeed a more modern and forward-looking India. He was called 'Mr Clean', and had made a good name by peacefully engaging with many of the secessionist situations. He also took on a rather progressive initiative in the cause of Muslim women, but quickly backtracked for fear of offending conservative Muslims. Then, as if to compensate, he attempted to please politicized Hindus by permitting the reopening of the disputed temple at Ayodhya. This was all the lead the Hindu nationalist parties needed, and they successfully used the issue of the temple at Ayodhya to move their politics to the centre stage of Indian democracy. As Khilnani notes, the rise of Hindu nationalism did not come from the 'primordial margins' of Indian society, but was stoked primarily by the urban elites, including Indira Gandhi (p. 54).

It was in the shadow of the growing visibility of the Ram Janmabhoomi movement and the chirpy middle-class consumerism of TV that, in 1987, Doordarshan began transmission of *Ramayan*. The decision to air the popular religious epic, it was noted, broke a 'Nehruvian taboo' on transmitting religious content on state television (A. Rajagopal, p. 35). On the contrary, *Ramayan* was described by the Director General of the Doordarshan of the time as a 'universal' story that embodied ideals of morality which were at the heart of Indian civilization. Although this approach may have shocked the elite intelligentsia, in the context of a popular Indian sensibility on matters of God, in itself it was perhaps not a serious violation of secularism as such. Secularism in India has often meant a fair regard for all religions rather than a denial of religion altogether. Furthermore, a legalistic enforcement of secularism in cultural expression in India is also virtually impossible, given the fact that many of its classical arts, including music and dance, are basically forms of either worship or storytelling about the gods. *Ramayan*, in this sense, was by no means an unexpected resurgence of some buried tradition. The story had been retold countless times, in films and in comic books, and was widely known, even among non-Hindus. How it was regarded may have varied—for some, it may have been just a story, and for many, a story about the gods. Its enduring existence and its plurality were testimony to the fact that the Ramayana's importance in South Asia far exceeded what anyone could do with it at any given time. However, in the years after *Ramayan* began airing, a broad transformation did indeed take place. To some extent, it may have been instigated politically; to some extent, it may have had to do with the form that it took on TV; but in any case, a new way of understanding also rose to prominence in India. It may not have replaced how one related to God as such, but it did sidle up to seemingly shadow the spiritual side altogether.

Ramayan and the rise of Hindu nationalism are perhaps

the most frequently examined topics in South Asian media studies. One persistent challenge in analysing these phenomena has, of course, been the need to acknowledge the importance of what we would, from a modern perspective, call 'faith' in the reception of shows such as this. At the outset, one must acknowledge that the spectacular popularity of *Ramayan* was about faith. Although the TV serials of the 1980s had indeed gathered regular audiences, what *Ramayan* achieved was simply unsurpassed. Every Sunday morning, it was often noted, the streets would be deserted. No event of any importance was ever scheduled during this hour. If there was a power failure at the time of its telecast, enraged fans might as well vent their anger on the electricity office. It was a national trance on a scale only reserved for very high-stakes cricket matches, but it was also deeply devotional. And despite the unfortunate electricity office building, the viewing of *Ramayan* was for the most part a rather peaceful and happy affair. A media researcher could walk into a stranger's apartment and ask if he could join them in watching the show (Rajagopal, p. 94). It left its viewers, as one of Rajagopal's subjects observed, with a 'cool mind' afterwards. In a country where aspirations were growing faster than the middle-class boom, and daily life was never free of struggle, it was an oasis of calm. *Ramayan* was received with due honour. Like the early cinema audiences of India, families often performed improvised religious rituals to mark the commencement of the show. People took a bath, lit their lamps and incense sticks, and watched quite devoutly. Was it the faith? Was it something really sublime? Was it the menacing advent of communalism, marching on the cultural trappings of a liberalizing economy with an ascendant middle class, masquerading as entertainment? A closer examination would perhaps serve to separate the myth (in the traditional sense) from the myths (in the political sense).

Ramayan was made by Ramanand Sagar, a Hindi film-maker who packed the serial with an eclectic mixture of elements drawn from Hindi cinema, North Indian folk tradition and American soap opera. Eclecticism in itself was not new in Indian popular culture, even in the mythologicals of the past. However, one key difference between the TV *Ramayan* and many of the earlier film versions was that on TV, and in the context of a modern middle-class sensibility veering towards a post-Nehruvian end, the eclecticism was claimed consciously by the serial as part of the story. Although critics often noted that *Ramayan* diminished the diversity of regional tellings of the tale by propagating a vast centralized one, the programme itself claimed to have drawn from a number of regional versions. Even if the claim came out of a noble Doordarshan sort of sentiment of promoting national integration ('Ek Ramayan, anek Ramayan', or 'one Ramayan, many Ramayans', one might have said of it perhaps, in the spirit of the famous Films Division short film *Ek Anek aur Ekta.*) and presenting it as a common part of Indian cultural heritage, it transformed what was essentially experienced as a story about gods into a story about the past. Unlike the classic mythological films, in which the story unfolded without preamble, the TV *Ramayan* was introduced from a perspective that took an epistemic advantage over the story itself. Mankekar (1999) writes:

> The very first episode used a combination of imagery and music to establish the purportedly pan-Indian character of the Ramayana. Early in its prologue, we see saints and poets

from all over India writing and singing passages from regional 'tellings' of the Ramayana. (p. 190)

Furthermore, as Rajagopal notes, the voice-over that introduced each episode sought to recast the story as a fundamentally human, rather than a Hindu, concern. Once again, given the tradition of universalism in India about religion, this might have been noble in intent, but in practice the effect was quite the opposite. Unlike the Ganeshas and yoga techniques that have travelled to the West as something not quite just Hindu any more, the humanistic emphasis of the serial's presentation (Rajagopal also notes that Tulsidas, whose version of the Ramayana is the dominant one, is portrayed here not as a saint but as a 'humanist educator') seems to call attention not so much to the universal ethical implications of a popular religious tradition—which are indeed relevant—but to an all-too-human emphasis of 'religion' over 'God'. In other words, the serial seems to be assuming a new, unprecedented position vis-à-vis popular experiences of religion—it is speaking from the authority of the modern nation, not unlike how other TV shows of the time, like the historic documentary *Discovery of India*, would. It is instructive that, as Rajagopal observes, Ashok Kumar— the veteran actor who introduced the show—is shown not in a temple or in a sacred place suggesting devotion, but in a library. *Ramayan*, it seems, was setting itself up to be part of a new discovery of India, on TV and for a modern, scientific age at that. It is perhaps not surprising, then, that what we find in Mankekar's ethnographic study of its viewers, for instance, is perhaps less of an engagement with the god Rama, and more of an appreciation of 'our heritage'. As one of her interviewees says, '*Ramayan* has taught us a lot about Hinduism . . . [and to be] proud of our heritage' (p. 181).

Even in itself, reimagining the Ramayana as a part of heritage and history may not be troubling, and neither would conflating 'Hindu' and 'Indian' in *some* contexts be. If a viewer thinks of *Ramayan* as both 'Indian' heritage and 'Hindu' heritage, that in itself need not be disenfranchising to the status of a non-Hindu Indian heritage, which is a great legacy as well. If the same viewer believes that Hindus and Muslims are not fundamentally different, it may also not be a bad thing to the extent that it marks a persistence of both a Gandhian and a Nehruvian sort of tolerance. However, as we see in some of the comments made by participants in Mankekar's study, there were already stereotypes and shortcuts circulating in the middle-class culture about the differences between Hindus and Muslims. Some of these were related to the sense of fear brought on and stoked by the rise of secessionism and terrorism, and some of them were more directly related to the propaganda points of the Hindu nationalist movement. In any case, the problem with the 'modern' preface with which *Ramayan* sought to unfold was more complex. To some extent, it was related to a warped sort of modernity, an attempt to reimagine the Ramayana not only as India's past, but as a past that was 'scientifically advanced' and rather curiously weaponized as well.

Rajagopal describes one episode in which two demons are conversing about the rishi (sage) whose ceremonies they are about to disrupt. They describe the actions of the sages as 'scientific experiments' which are the source of the 'Aryans'' strength. Elsewhere, the rishi Vishwamitra tells his pupil Ram about the weapons that he has acquired through 'worldly, heavenly and scientific research'. The reinvention of the rishis—who in the earlier films and comics were portrayed as wise, philosophical and mostly harmless—as ancient Indian proto-scientists engaged in 'research', which inevitably involves the production of weapons, strikes an uncanny resemblance to the middle-class climate of the 1980s, with its aspirations to upward mobility through education, computers and science. It also parallels a growing sense of Hinduism as 'scientific' in a somewhat Darwinian manner that Rajagopal notes is 'suspiciously similar to the parable of conquest by the West' (p. 107). The problem with this emerging ideology is not whether Hinduism is or is not 'scientific', but why a great religion should be sought to be reinstated in esteem by recourse through the touchstone of science. Was it not enough to think of Rama as great and an ideal example? Did we need justification on the terms of modern-day knowledge as well? The modernist retelling of the Ramayana extends beyond its proto-IIT ashrams to questions of political identity as well. As Rajagopal writes, in *Ramayan* the conflict between good and evil—once defined largely in terms of conduct and character, and not identity and evolutionary status—was closer to a modern rivalry between nations in various stages of development. The conversation of the demons, he notes, is less like the malicious chatter of noisy troublemakers, and instead suggests more of 'the uncomprehending hostility of a less civilized people towards a superior culture' (p. 105). Given the close overlapping of modern notions of science, progress and development in the new form, it is not surprising perhaps that one participant in Rajagopal's study writes: '[T]he language of the dialogue is most scientific, most expressive, most soothing, most natural, and has achieved the task of directly entering my heart' (p. 137).

For a show with a modern, almost Nehruvian tone in its

rationality, to lead up to responses that wed science and feeling in such an uncanny manner may seem strange. Clearly, the pretence to universalism and modern certitudes with which the show begins is not associated with an equally universal exploration of the Ramayana as a statement on the human condition (like Peter Brook's version of the Mahabharata, perhaps). Following its somewhat historicist preamble, the show turns profoundly into a devotionalist rendition that borders on hagiography. Unlike some of the old films about gods and saints, the televised *Ramayan* did not just leave devotionalism to the audience, but cultivated it consciously in its narrative and techniques. Proceeding at a 'glacial pace', it dwelt slowly and intensely on moments of emotional interaction signified by the use of extended and very tight close-ups. It was not enough to convey a mood with a song and a gesture or two. If Shabari tasted the fruit before offering it to Ram, or if his brother Bharat took his sandals, or if one of many other incidents long familiar to audiences happened, the reactions were staged carefully as well. Rajagopal describes these scenes vividly and quotes a critic who calls the phenomenon of soap-opera style close-ups in the series 'reaction mania' (p. 116).

The mixture of modern aspiration, selective revisionism, nostalgia for a Golden Age, melodrama, self-conscious devotionalism and middle-class hopes for a consumerist future created an experience around *Ramayan* which may not have replaced altogether the deeper views of God that have existed in the popular culture, but certainly relegated the ways of relating to religion that existed in the media of the past. Whether this experience reflected the growing Hindu nationalist movement, or strengthened it, it may be too soon to say even two decades after the serial was aired. There have been numerous mythological serials after *Ramayan*, including a grand *Mahabharat* on Doordarshan shortly after, and numerous regional-language ones on satellite channels as well. There has also been a general proliferation of pop religion since, with music videos and film songs playing up a visually recognizable youth culture rooted in Hindu sensibilities. Young men and women wear 'Om' tattoos and T-shirts depicting gods, or saffron robes, and sing and chant in a playful fashion. Of course, by 2005, Hanuman had also become an animated character and a stuffed toy that children bought at one of the many malls in the country. Politically, Hindu nationalism peaked in its aggressive form in the early 1990s (with some notable regional exceptions), which were marked by the razing of the disputed mosque, bloody riots between Hindus and Muslims, and violent bomb blasts directed against the citizens of Bombay. In 1998, a BJP-led coalition took power at the Centre, which it held until 2004. Regardless of its political fortunes and the actual (im)probability of its goal of establishing a 'Hindu state', the Hindu nationalist movement certainly achieved one cultural transformation by the end of the 1980s—it created a modern, political Hindu identity and a vision of the nation as a homeland for Hindus in a world with religions hostile to Hinduism. It did this at great cost. Its consequence, though, for how India sees itself may be better explored in a more global context, to which I turn in the following chapter. Suffice it to say that Sagar's *Ramayan* had one more element that none of the old classics did. It did not demonize Muslims or others, and it was perhaps felt for the most part as a religious tale; but it did show a scene in which Ram, in exile, prays to a clod of earth that he has carried with him from the place of his birth. No black-and-white NTR Ramayana would have thought of things like that.

No Direction?

If, in the early 1980s, TV was thought of as a handy tool to keep people indoors when 'communally sensitive' events were taking place, no such panacea would be possible against the onslaught of political violence that would take place by the end of the decade. The 1989 elections took place in the wake of a decade of regional and religious politics. In spite of having started with a massive sympathy vote and a reputation as Mr Clean, Rajiv Gandhi's alleged involvement in an arms-pay-off scandal led to a single pointed campaign against the Congress as a corrupt party. In the lead-up to the election, it was not just the Hindu nationalist parties but an array of new and rising political parties, riding a wave of public anger against corruption. Despite another dramatic advertising campaign warning of the dangers to India from secessionism, the Congress could not convince voters against their belief that the system had become so corrupt that only change would please them. It did not matter, of course, what direction the change would take—some voted for their regional parties, some for the Left, some for the breakaway parties of ex-Congress leaders, some for the rising caste-based parties and some for the BJP. Because of an electoral arrangement by these parties, the Congress did not win a clear majority, despite having won the most seats. There were some rumours that Rajiv Gandhi would, like his mother once before, proclaim an Emergency. It was not to be, and it seemed that what he sought was vindication once again from the electorate.

In retrospect, if *Ramayan* had any political consequence, it was less in terms of helping the BJP win and more in unseating Rajiv Gandhi. The story, despite its various narrative reinventions, was widely perceived as a critique of power—of how people in power had become arrogant, greedy and thieving, and how only a radical change could replace the rule of the corrupt with the rule of 'Ram', in this context with middle-class goodies for all. In 1989, when only the second non-Congress government in post-Independence India took power, it was supported by both the BJP and the Left. For a few months, there was no talk of a Hindu nation or of liberating Rama's birthplace. However, in July 1990, in a daring move that some called progressive and others thought explosive, Prime Minister V.P. Singh unlocked the Mandal Commission Report, which would increase the share of jobs and seats in government and colleges 'reserved' for a category called the Other Backward Castes. Middle-class students not entitled to such benefits protested and began to immolate themselves. A no-confidence vote was called against V.P. Singh and his government collapsed. A caretaker government was then installed with the support of the Congress, which would last only a few months. Meanwhile, working against the threat of 'Mandal' to the upper-caste Hindu base, the BJP leader L.K. Advani revived the issue of the 'Mandir' and began a tour of the country on an improvised 'rath' (chariot), leaving a trail of violence. The Hindu nationalist movement rose to prominence on its promise to 'liberate' the birthplace of Lord Ram, fed by a variety of cultural forces, enabled not in the least by the proliferation of media and consumer culture.

At the time of the mid-term elections of 1991, a different

sort of 'homeland' issue came back to take a fatal toll. A suicide bomber of the LTTE, the Tamil separatist movement in Sri Lanka, assassinated Rajiv Gandhi while he was campaigning near Madras. A Congress government was voted to power, largely on the strength of sympathy for Rajiv Gandhi; and while it prepared to deal with economic compulsions both domestic and foreign, the identity politics of the earlier decade finally reached a crescendo on 6 December 1992, when the troubled and troubling mosque was razed to the ground by a mob, as various leaders of the Hindu nationalist movement watched. In the year to come, riots and vicious bomb blasts would maul the city of Bombay. Also, around the same time, yet another homeland struggle was turning increasingly violent. In Kashmir, the proliferation of what was called cross-border terrorism was increasing, with Kashmiri Muslims turning viciously against the state's minority Hindu population. As Guha writes, the two developments raised serious concerns about the future of Hindus and Muslims in India: 'Would one trust a state that could not honor its commitment to protect an ancient place of worship? Would one trust a community that so brutally expelled those of a different faith?' This trust would be tested again in the coming decade, but as a much bigger picture unfolded, of which a media boom was an integral part, many attempts to restore this trust would also be made, not in the least by a resurgent film industry. As they entered the age of globalization, both India and its media would both embark on a profound reimagination of almost everything discussed thus far.

4

WORLD

Baywatch
Channel V
MTV
'Made in India'
Hum Aapke Hain Koun..!
Indian
Mission Kashmir
Company
Lage Raho Munna Bhai

INDIA, IT MAY BE SAID, HAS BEEN MORE *IN* THE WORLD THAN *OF* IT. FOR a country that has attracted visitors and invaders over the centuries (including one who didn't quite get there but instead found an antipodal landmass where many Indians like to live these days), it has not perhaps particularly made an effort to get to know the rest of the world. On the good side, this lack of expansive curiosity may be related to one fact that Non-resident Indians are quite proud of reiterating—that India does not have a history of conquering foreign countries. At the same time, modern India is undoubtedly fascinated by the outside world, and the West in particular. A large measure of that fascination is somewhat narcissistic and aspirational. India wants to be like the West, in some ways, but it also wants to be what it thinks the West thinks of as India—the land of good values, traditions and spirituality, which is also of late becoming a knowledge superpower. It has not forgotten completely that the West did behave poorly with India too, but that part seems to be less relevant these days, as prime ministers go to England and say nice things about the time it ruled India. Such nice gestures also extend to Indians abroad, who are now regularly feted by the government for their successes and their services. Foreign visitors are most welcome, whether their purpose is education, business, health care or religion (buying and selling).

The great exchange of people and things between India and the world that has so quickly become a reality since the

1990s may seem unremarkable for the hundreds of millions who were born after this time; but in the bigger temporal context of post-Independence India, it was indeed a staggering, and somewhat sudden, transformation. Even if its seeds were sown long before, the advent of globalization in India since 1991 marked a new dimension, not only in the history of the country but also in how it would see itself. The 1990s were the decade of an unsurpassed media boom in India. Cable and satellite TV channels proliferated rapidly, and so did their viewers, growing by tens of millions each year. Despite some initial concern, Indian cinema did not falter in the face of global TV, but found a new resurgence with a different sort of audience as it emerged in the Indian diaspora abroad, as well as in the new malls and multiplexes of urban India. As the media flourished at the global, national, regional and local levels, so did the stories that they told about what it meant to be a part of the world.

The story of India's encounter with globalization has unfolded in numerous forms in the films and TV programmes of recent years. Even if not all of these have engaged explicitly with the world outside India, many recent themes in films and TV programmes may be interpreted, directly or indirectly, as a response to the social changes brought by globalization to India. In this chapter, I offer such an interpretation using a number of examples. I begin with a brief discussion of the history of political and economic thinking (and its cinematic parallels) about India's place in the world from the time of Independence to the moment of liberalization in 1991. I then turn to the media and globalization with a discussion of the somewhat sudden invasion by Star TV and its flagship show *Baywatch* in the early 1990s, and the mixture of surprise and acceptance it found in India. Following this, I consider more closely the dominant theme about globalization that emerged in the popular Indian media story, using my own study of MTV and Channel V audiences in the later part of the decade. In the fourth section, I focus on some of the themes that have come to mark Indian cinema in the last decade, including the notion of the family in *Hum Aapke Hain Koun..!* and the changing concept of identity in *Kuch Kuch Hota Hai* (1998). I also address the growing celebration of the figure of the Non-resident Indian (NRI) in the films of this period. In the final two sections, I turn respectively to the questions of violence and non-violence in Indian cinema. Since the 1990s, violence has grown from being merely one more element in the cinematic formula to an explicit predilection in the themes of many new films, whether gangster films like *Company* (2002) or films about terrorism like *Mission Kashmir*. I discuss these films with the aim of exploring not what effect they may have on real-life violence, but simply as a way of evaluating what sort of a moral sensibility we may still find in our popular cinematic tales about violence and its uses. On that note, I also examine the phenomenon of 'Gandhigiri' in the wake of the film *Lage Raho Munna Bhai* (2006) and the persistent but sometimes confusing relevance of Mahatma Gandhi, and the ideal of ahimsa, to the land of its birth as it enters the twenty-first century.

India and the World: From Independence to Liberalization

For a region that had been at the centre of world trade in the first half of the last millennium, India was understandably insular, at least in an economic sense, in its early post-

Independence years. Although certain international
sentiments, especially in terms of anti-colonial solidarity,
were in evidence in efforts like the Non-Alignment Movement,
the period after Independence was marked more by ideals
like self-sufficiency and concerns about sovereignty rather
than those of free trade. This was by no means the result of
xenophobia or nativism, for even at the height of the freedom
struggle, Gandhi's critique was of Western industrial
'civilization' (not yet a good idea, he might have said) and
not of the English people as such. Both Gandhi and Nehru, in
their own ways, embodied a certain kind of universalism
in their thinking about India and the world. However, when
it came to India's interests, especially in economic terms,
neither were of the view that it lay outside the
country. Gandhi had been an advocate of 'Swadeshi'—a
philosophy of self-sustenance—while Nehru's faith in
modernization did not quite extend all the way to a complete
embrace of Western prescriptions for progress. Khilnani
(1999) writes:

> The one insight from Nehru's intellectual engagements of
> the 1930s that he never abandoned was the Marxist analysis
> of imperialism, which had convinced him as accurate about
> the economic relationship between colonizer and colonized.
> (p. 76)

Nehruvian India thus remained committed to a path of
economic independence. What it meant in the daily lives of
Indians was that there were few of the pleasures of foreign
brands for them to enjoy. Consumerism, especially the
consumption of foreign goods, was seen as both an individual
and a national luxury. It was an era of 'conspicuous frugality'

as Kaviraj calls it (1998) and it would more or less prevail until the 1980s. However, it was not only the economic dimension which would shape Indian perceptions of the world at the time. Nehru's vision for India and its place in the world also included a political stand. Despite the temptation among some Indian elites to pursue closer ties with America, and the concern among others about the possible effects of American materialism on India, Nehru's position ultimately emerged in favour of what was, at least in principle, a third position in the Cold War. As Guha writes, Nehru saw Non-Alignment as more than merely an escape from having to take sides in the Cold War. Instead, he saw in it a possibility for a 'salutary moderating effect on the hubris of the great powers' (p. 172).

The Bandung Conference of 1955 took place at a time when many nations were still under colonial rule. In this sense, the vision shared by Nehru and his counterparts was rooted in a reality of the time. The project of decolonization was hardly complete. However, Non-Alignment, and especially India's role in it, was also tested in the coming years by the repercussions that the Cold War was having over the world. The United States had, as early as 1954, signed a pact providing arms to Pakistan, precipitating perhaps the beginnings of a certain amount of apprehension in India about the West. As Andrew Rotter (2000) writes, the relationship between the US and Pakistan was guided not only by geopolitical calculations but also by the beliefs and prejudices of Washington's conservative elites with regard to the Hindu and the Muslim religions, cultures and even dietary habits. This uneasy relationship between the three countries would exist until the 1990s and, directly or indirectly, play into the Indian fears of the 'foreign hand' from time to time. The economic and political realities of India in the global context also found expression in various ways in the films of the Nehru and Indira Gandhi periods. Even if a streetwise sort of cosmopolitanism was in evidence as early as the 1950s, when Raj Kapoor proclaimed his Hindustani heart amidst an array of foreign sartorial objects (admittedly tattered as would befit a tramp), there was also a fair measure of fear and suspicion of the West as a source of moral and cultural corruption in some films. The films of Manoj Kumar, for example, 'indulge(d) in national chauvinism, contrasting son-of-the-soil goodness with Western evil' (A. Rajadhyaksha and P. Willemen, 1999, p. 133). The stereotype of the Western vamp was seen all too often in the films of this period, and the dazzling Helen often played roles that were ambiguously foreign in implication (Jerry Pinto, 2006). By the 1970s, another foreign stereotype was added to the rogues' gallery of Indian cinema—the Arab sheikh—who was not only a favourite character in walk-on roles but also, it seems, a favourite disguise for the hero to wear while infiltrating the villain's lair. It is also no surprise, perhaps, that the most common occupation for villains in the films of the 1970s was to be a 'smuggler'. The violators of Indian borders and the notoriously acronymized laws like COFEPOSA (Conservation of Foreign Exchange and Prevention of Smuggling Act) were deemed quite reprehensible in the films of those days, and often found themselves defeated by the hero's fists despite their obvious wealth, power and Vat 69 bottle décor. It is interesting that Indian cinema seldom engaged with foreign characters (or actors) in any sustained manner at this time.

One exception, at least in Telugu, was the 1987 film *Padamati Sandhya Ragam* (The West's song of dusk), which was an unlikely hit. It featured a romance between a Telugu woman and a white American man, and featured many images of the life of Telugu doctors in the American suburbs.

Even if the West was seen as a source of concern in Indian films, it also enjoyed the lure of the elusive, particularly among Indian middle classes. American media were restricted to occasional films which arrived in Indian theatres years after their release abroad, and perhaps the only American TV show featured on Doordarshan before the 1980s was *The Lucy Show*. The first influx of global culture, in a sense, came to India during the limited liberalization of the economy in the early 1980s. The VCR boom of this time led to a spate of video libraries and 'parlours' across the country. For the first time, American films were available on tape days after their release abroad. TV shows like *Dallas* and *Top of the Pops* were available at the video libraries. In time Doordarshan also slowly increased its foreign programming, broadcasting shows like *Star Trek* and Carl Sagan's *Cosmos* on the national network on Sunday mornings. By the end of the decade, Doordarshan also began *The World This Week*, which struck a chord with the growing global aspirations of the middle class.

Globalization, in a much larger sense, would find its way into India in the 1990s. The economic policies of the 1980s, including the drive towards consumer-oriented growth, coupled with the political tensions and violent disturbances of Mandal and Mandir, had placed India's foreign reserves in a precarious situation. This was also compounded by the impact that the Gulf War had on the remittances sent home by Indian workers. By the early 1990s, 'economic reforms'

seemed the best way forward, and Prime Minister P.V.
Narasimha Rao's government initiated these measures at this
time (under the guidance of the then Finance Minister and
present Prime Minister Manmohan Singh). Liberalization
involved deregulation and disinvestment, privatization,
limited opening up of Indian markets to foreign investment
and, of course, one important response (or lack thereof) to a
tremendous technological leap that came from China—the
rise of Star TV.

In 1992, Hong-Kong-based Star TV began broadcasting
across Asia, and the few channels that were available led to a
frenzied, unregulated effort to receive it in India. In the
matter of a few years, millions of households were connected
via cable run up by neighbourhood entrepreneurs (usually
the local toughs) to satellite dishes, and to the dazzling world
of satellite TV. The state had neither the vision nor the will to
respond, except to further commercialize Doordarshan when
a rival channel—the Hindi-language Zee TV—began
broadcasting as well. Although the early Star TV had carried
mainly Western programming (American soaps, BBC news,
some MTV), by the late 1990s, satellite TV in India had
localized and proliferated. Indian cinema, despite initial fears
about the satellite invasion, had found a new lease of life as
the main source of programming for many channels, and as
always, provided a vision for India to think about its new
place in the world.

The Whole World is *Baywatch*ing

The effect of the coming of satellite TV to India in the early
1990s may be summed up in one word—normalization.
Simply put, a lot of things which may have at first seemed

new, strange, disturbing even, all became a part of the domestic and inner landscape of Indian television audiences in the matter of a few years. In terms of rapidity and intensity, the advent of satellite television in India was probably one of the most striking examples of cultural transformation anywhere in the world. However, as the Star TV phenomenon spread rapidly in the early 1990s, there was an occasional sense of unease perhaps, but it never mounted to anything like full-blown opposition of either a cultural or political sort. Notwithstanding the occasional public demonstrations of nationalist anger at Valentine's Day cards in later years, the wider reaction in India to the coming of global TV was one of accommodation rather than resistance.

Such resistance might have been expected on at least two grounds. Although the national and cultural sovereignty argument with all its concerns about Star TV as an agent of cultural imperialism made the rounds in intellectual circles for a while, the broader middle-class attitude seemed to welcome it on a more pragmatic point like the importance of news and information for careers and advancement. The second ground on which the new world of satellite TV might have been potentially troubling to Indian viewers was its rather promiscuous imagery. The images that were being beamed into millions of Indian households by the early 1990s were full of exactly the sort of Western lifestyles and habits some of the patriotic Hindi films of the 1950s had feared. These images were fundamentally of bodies—sculpted, glamorized, nearly naked, mostly blonde and, of course, highly sexualized. Whether these were on *Baywatch*, *The Bold and the Beautiful* or the hip-hop music videos of MTV, these were all now inside Indian homes, stuck like house guests destined never to leave, forcing the awkwardness they caused to parents, grandparents and children watching them to sort itself out and disappear instead.

The question of 'vulgarity' was, of course, not completely absent from public concerns in India. Indian films were often criticized around this time for their seeming capitulation to the prurient tastes of the 'masses'. There was certainly a sensibility that existed prior to the satellite-TV age about what was and what was not considered 'acceptable'. While the permissive tales and explicit imagery of satellite TV might have been theoretically 'unacceptable' in such a sense, perhaps they were not entirely shocking to Indian sensibilities, given that these were mostly of foreign origin. It might have been easy to hold doubts about propriety at bay by assuming that it was only to be expected that *Baywatch* would feature blonde women in beach clothes. It was, after all, the oldest expectation about the West that existed among Indian audiences. However, the really incredible leap of normalization took place in the period following the first wave of global TV in India, when Indian TV channels began to rise as well, and some of them had no qualms apparently about following the *Baywatch* and *Santa Barbara* models of bodily exposure and conduct. As journalist Amrita Shah (1997) writes, on one Hindi entertainment channel, a compère dressed in a traditional sari asked male guests about their libido, while another mainstream channel thought nothing of broadcasting pornography on Saturday nights. Even Doordarshan, she notes, got into the fray with 'double entendres and suggestive gyrations' (p. 134).

It is easy to see the criticism of examples such as these as one that comes invariably from a prudish conservatism, but that is not necessarily the case here. The breaking of many hitherto-inviolable cultural borders of decency in the early 1990s did not take place from any sort of well-considered ideology about society, relationships, freedom or responsibility. It merely happened in the same manner that much of the satellite-TV boom happened—unanticipated, unregulated and clearly unabashed. It does merit a consideration of why it took the forms it did, and why there was seemingly so little resistance to it. This is not to say that the new forms of entertainment were welcomed wholeheartedly by everyone. There were complaints, letters in the TV Guide supplements that now came with newspapers and even some memorable incidents, like the decision made by the residents of a colony in Bombay to rid themselves of TV altogether. However, for the most part, it may be said that all that was lurid simply turned into air—unnoticed, pervasive, everywhere.

One reason for the developments of the early 1990s is fairly obvious. In the rapidly changing political environment of the period, the government simply did not have the will or the vision to respond in any coherent manner to the coming of satellite TV and the literal uprising of dishes and cable networks on the ground to meet it. In the spirit of economic liberalization which demanded a welcoming approach towards enterprise in all its forms, perhaps scrutiny and regulation were not exactly popular ideals for the authorities at the time. In any case, in the absence of any sort of policy or enforcement about satellite and cable TV, its spread took place in India on the instincts and muscles of raw enterprise. The dawn of the most pervasive and intrusive new medium in India's history was heralded not by media visionaries or even professionals, but by entrepreneurs in the broadest sense.

As Shah once again notes, the satellite TV bandwagon came to include producers and investors with little expertise, such as 'shop owners, housewives, sundry exporters, real estate agents, newspaper hacks, etc.' (p. 132). Although in a few years the talented and professional would also make a mark, the content of the new Indian satellite TV channels and their forms of distribution (cable would remain a largely local and at times even violently competitive enterprise) came about with few considerations about quality, and perhaps decency even.

A second and perhaps more subtle issue with the normalization of the new forms of TV had to do with the sort of thinking that grew around its reception. The new TV environment was seemingly democratic, particularly in contrast to what had been perceived as the stately elitism of Doordarshan. Its anchors spoke 'Hinglish' or its regional equivalents instead of formal and well-bordered languages of any previously known sort. They dressed more casually, and moved their limbs about a lot more than any newsreader had before them. The titles of the shows and the ever-increasing torrent of advertising seemed to address the viewer directly, in easy intimacy, as if 'you' were the only person on earth who mattered, and the pursuit of 'your' pleasure the only thing on earth that mattered. However, despite all the democratic, easy-going American-style first-name-basis posturing, TV was still associated in India, like any public medium, with authority. If something was on TV, then it had to be important, even the most preposterous claims of infomercials, for example. The new contents of TV were seen not simply as a statement against authority, with all the risks that might entail, but simply as fully acceptable because they would not have been on TV had they been any other way. Shah quotes an advertising executive and mother of three:

> As far as Star [TV] was concerned it united most families in the feeling that what they were watching was not part of 'our' culture. But with an Indian cast doing the same thing that gap disappeared ... No one can deny that the new Hindi film songs are extremely obscene, yet *the fact that they are on television somehow conveys the impression that someone has deemed them okay for us to watch.* (pp. 134–35, emphasis added)

That sort of quiet assumption of authority for whatever now passed for normal on TV is perhaps what made it possible for the sort of incredible contradictions that came to be more or less settled in the popular perception of India and the world in the years that followed. The experience of globalization in India essentially began with a moment of perplexed voyeurism and went from there into a formidable story about identity and global ambition. This story, as I show in the following section, reinvented many assumptions about being Indian. Globalization would be seen not as a foreign invasion into India, but as the opposite. Being assertive (or 'attitude-y' perhaps) would be seen as the hallmark for a young generation that could flaunt this skill in not only professional settings but increasingly in personal relations and in identity-exclamations as well. The story of globalization, by the late 1990s, would be in a much more complex form than what the early days of satellite television could have foretold. But one last example may be worth retelling, since it is not especially fashionable to think of 1991 as a moment of 'conquest' except in rather dour circles of political thought.

One day, around the time I was doing my field work for

my dissertation in the late 1990s, I visited a school which was celebrating Independence Day. For hours, hundreds of little boys and girls dressed in smart whites had showed off their talent in a most disciplined manner. They marched, they sang, they chanted prayers, they gave speeches and they made me feel as optimistic as I do when I watch an Indian film these days (I must add that, in those days, I was exceptionally pessimistic, as indeed was the lot of a graduate student in a leftist tradition). Perhaps my optimism was also related to the fact that, as someone who had been away from the country in a time of rapid change, it was endearing to see some things, like school ceremonies, remain quite the same as they had been in the time of my own schooldays. But suddenly, as the ceremonies officially concluded, the event turned into an impromptu party. An A.R. Rahman hit came on the loudspeakers and the huge field turned into a dancing frenzy of little white bodies, which was still nice to the eye. But then, among the dance moves that many of these children made was what Indian polite society calls the 'pelvic thrust'. I found the sight of small children pseudo-sexualized before their time ramming their tiny mid-sections into the air grotesque and dismal. But this is what TV had done, and as I was later told, parents had gone along with it. It had become common practice for adults to tell their children to 'show uncle and aunty your dance', and this what the children would do, as guests and hosts tried to keep a straight face. This is the sort of moment that inevitably reminded me of the gloomy Naipaul. I cannot imagine what it was like for great cities like Hampi to have been razed by conquest; but in my time, this sight of dozens of little boys feigning sexual thrusting to each other in view of their teachers and parents, as the sun set once more over the Deccan, will do. In time, India may have made globalization its own to a certain extent, and seeing it as a 'fall' in any sense may now seem harsh. But I like to record that moment for what it is, because it does remind us that sometimes we do slip. Liberalization may have been an economic imperative in 1991, but a virtue was made not just of necessity, but of vice as well, to put it bluntly. What was once unthinkable, it seemed, had become inevitable overnight, and even commendable a few hours later.

Made in India

Even if the early period of satellite TV was marked by the triumph of voyeurism over vision, by the mid-1990s, a story of sorts about globalization began to form in the media. The wriggling and writhing bodies of music videos and film songs did not quite disappear, but turned less conspicuous perhaps because these were now subsumed within a larger narrative about the new global experience that Indians were going through. Uncannily, if globalization had seemed like a simple process of 'invasion' in the early years when Star TV and foreign brands were coming into the country, it now seemed to be more about India going out to take on the world and take its rightful place in it as well. The anthem of globalization in India, albeit in the pop music video idiom, was the song 'Made in India' by Alisha Chinai. It captured much of what globalization in India now seemed to be about; it was not the once somewhat feared loss of culture, but the opposite, a resurgent, in-your-face, globally competitive nationalism. That was the story that the media were putting out on a fairly widespread basis, and it certainly resonated with audiences as well.

In just about half a decade since Star TV entered India, a full-fledged boom was under way. Not only had cable and satellite connections grown by tens of millions of households each year but so had the number of channels that were now operating. An urban family with a connection could now receive channels that were local, regional, national and international in their language and reach. The simple process of 'Westernization' or 'cultural imperialism' that media observers once feared had proved somewhat more complex, with the rise of Indian satellite channels like Eenadu TV and the localization strategies of foreign-owned networks like Star as well. Not only were there more channels and programmes in Hindi and Indian regional languages than in English, most of these programmes were also based on Indian films and film songs, disproving yet again some initial fears about what satellite TV might do to cinema. The global media, it seemed, came to India, and decided to go local.

The 'Indianization' of global media, so to speak, began with Channel V. In 1994, Star TV began transmitting a music TV channel that was quite similar to MTV, but with an important difference. Channel V was strikingly local. Its self-conscious, idiosyncratic Indian English slogan 'V are like this only' embodied everything it hoped to be. It had the 'feel' of global TV, with hip VJs, pop music, swaying cameras, catchy editing and quirky promos, but its content was largely Indian. It played Indian film songs and pop songs presented by foreign-Indian VJs and, most vividly, turned Indian everyday life into an object of style and parody. For the first time, TV was full of things that had not been on TV before—chai sellers, people spitting paan, elephants in the street, roadside hair salons, auto rickshaws—all the things that 'real' India had which Doordarshan had never really noticed, and certainly not in this way. One of the most popular figures in the nascent youth culture of this time was Quick Gun Murugan, a Channel V promo character based loosely on the cowboy heroes of a certain kind of 1970s' Tamil cinema. He was deadly, devastating and consumed dosas with panache. A few years later, an 'election entrepreneur' called Udham Singh became a popular host—the euphemism was a reference to his occupation. He was a village thug who beat up people and helped 'rig' elections. He also introduced global stars like Madonna and the Spice Girls in his own rustic style.

Channel V essentially created a new sensibility for the young about being Indian. I recalled the sense of watching it for the first time in 1995 and thinking that everything on it looked like India, but it looked as if someone else was looking at it. In other words, it was not the visual culture of Doordarshan or Indian cinema. It was a new regime of visual representation, so to speak, and it made the familiar seem exotic. Why this happened was a combination of marketing strategy and creativity. The Indian TV audience was not large enough or segmented enough to sustain a fully independent youth-oriented music channel. Most households in India at that time had a single TV set, which meant that the rebellion of youth culture and music TV had to be tempered by a consideration for the older family members in the room as well. This led to a unique intergenerational approach, wherein the channel was positioned as a 'family channel in demographics, but a youth channel in attitude'. Finally, one more important consideration prevailed. Localization had already been seen as a necessity in a market where even the middle classes were rooted in Indian languages and film culture, and pop music was a tiny portion of the market. Channel V took a leap in including film music in its programming, and essentially told its young urban middle-class viewers that Indian film music was 'really cool' (quoted in S. Hussain, 1997). Indian music TV came to be dominated by Indian film songs (with some Indian pop and Western pop thrown in), but with 'attitude', a sensibility that made everything different from the old Doordarshan shows. Channel V was so successful in reaching its audience that, when MTV India began broadcasting, it too followed a path of 'Indianization'. Ironically, five years after the 'satellite invasion', it seemed that each global media company was trying to be more 'Indian' than the other. It was as if globalization was not an invasion, but really about the world trying to woo India as it strode confidently on to the world stage. And appropriately enough, it was in the ever-popular form of the music video that the slogan of the decade emerged: 'Made in India'.

Alisha Chinai's 'Made in India' was not only a commercial success, reaching sales levels which Indian pop had never quite seen before, but also the first song to have had a music video formally made to promote it. The video tells the story of a princess who is wooed by a number of suitors from various parts of the world. She turns them all down. Finally, just as she is about to lose hope, her dream suitor arrives, duly fetched into the royal court in a box labelled 'Made in India'. I interviewed a number of young middle-class viewers a few years after this song first appeared, and found that it had touched a sense of national pride in them about finally being recognized on a global scale. They saw the video as a sign of India being able to make things that would now sell in a competitive marketplace, not the least music videos themselves. Globalization, it seemed, was now being seen not merely as foreign goods or culture coming into India, but interpreted instead as being about India going abroad to take on the world through its products, services, people and culture.

The theme of India becoming a part of the world was a pervasive one in the media of the time, spanning film songs, music videos and advertisements. But the question must be asked whether this theme was portrayed and, more importantly, understood, in an accurate manner. If we look more closely at some of the imagery that was used to construct this pervasive sense of global-Indianness in the media, we find many troubling elements. 'Made in India' is full of orientalist images like snake charmers and wild animals, as if the whole scene was out of some nineteenth-century European fantasy about India. The promos of MTV and Channel V highlighted exactly the sort of thing that might catch the eye of the foreign tourist but pass unnoticed in the daily lives of Indians. The voice-overs on these channels were delivered invariably in a foreign accent, with even Indian names being pronounced the way perhaps Americans would. The sights and sounds of TV, it seemed, were conspiring to conjure up an illusion of global culture for India that wasn't quite rooted in reality. It was, therefore, perhaps not surprising that some of the participants in my study seemed to think that the same shows they were watching on MTV were being watched by viewers all around the world.

But there was one important way in which audiences were thinking about themselves which perhaps exceeded the superficialities or fantasies of these new tall tales of globalization in the popular culture. The songs they liked may have all been too bluntly nationalistic ('East or West, India Is the Best' and 'I Love My India'), but their interpretations of what it meant to be Indian, or global, suggested sensibilities that were closer to the universalism and cosmopolitanism of the earlier phases of Indian cinema, rather than the visual clichés of the new culture. The participants in my study would frequently describe globalization, and being Indian, in terms of families, friends and relationships, rather than in terms of commerce and material success. As one participant said about 'Made in India': 'When you see the song, the feeling comes . . . that among all the husbands in the world, it is the Indian husband who loves the most' (Juluri, 2003, p. 99). Such a claim may seem merely like a Guinness Book of Records sort of aspiration brought into the terrain of relationships, but is not necessarily so. For people with such a strong and confident sense of being Indian and global, my participants did not blindly claim some sort of Indian moral superiority. As the following exchange about the logic of Alisha's choice in 'Made in India' suggests, two high-school students in my study show quite an open mind:

> Student One: There are many people outside who have a much better heart than Indians.
>
> Student Two: It's not compulsory that an Indian's heart is only good. You know, a foreigner can be much better than an Indian. It doesn't matter which place you are (from), it's the character that's important. (p. 101)

The lyrics of the song do set it up in such a way that the heroine of unspecified nationality considers the suitors carefully and finally picks the Indian, not just because he is Indian, but because he has the right sort of heart. In this manner, there is a sense in which the pop patriotism of music TV is also buffered with a sense of open-mindedness, not unlike the many Indian film songs of yore which celebrated the trustiness of the heart over superficial things like the colour of one's skin, or one's status and class and caste. Interestingly, on the question of marriage, it was not so much the triumph of an Indian man with a fairy-tale princess that was mentioned by participants as an example of India's successful globalization, but the real-life actions of Indians abroad. By the mid 1990s, the Non-resident Indian had become a widely feted figure in the Indian media. The government set up a ministry for NRIs and PIOs (People of Indian Origin), and started an annual celebration to honour them. The success of NRIs became a topic of widespread admiration as well. The rise of the diasporic audiences also led to an increase in the figure of the NRI in Indian cinema (which I discuss in the next section), but what is worth appreciating, from the point of view of India's first generation of global audiences who were imagining their place in the world, is that they thought of their people first, even in an age of ridiculous caricatures and careering consumerism. The greatest triumph of India in globalization, at least according to one participant in my study, was that 'People are going and settling outside India and they are searching for a counterpart made in India' (p. 109). Indians could go abroad and become successful, but still come home, so to speak. Their hearts, after all, as the song had reminded everyone, were still made in India.

Friends, Families and Foreign Locations

Indian cinema's first major response to the rapid and sweeping changes brought on by globalization and satellite TV was a massive three-hour pretence that nothing had changed in India. The only signs of the globalization that we see in *Hum Aapke Hain Koun..!* (henceforth *HAHK*) are a bottle of Pepsi (from which Tuffy the dog drinks, using a straw at that) and a reference to a character's business trip abroad to set up a foreign collaboration for his younger brother. Otherwise, *HAHK*, as its viewers noted with the sort of inevitable and inexhaustible smile the very mention of its name evoked, was just a film about a wedding; and yet it was so much about what was happening in India at the time. There was no other film like it. It did not have any of the violence and vulgarity that had made middle-class and family audiences begin to avoid Hindi films in general. It did not even have a story in a typical sense, and was described by some viewers as nothing more than a wedding video. Its story is simple. There is a big, happy, wealthy joint family full of people who eat and laugh and play together as weddings unfold. The festive mood in the film is what is paramount, and the scenes just follow somewhere below, and mostly entail singing and celebrating various social and religious ceremonies before, during and after the wedding.

Yet, this seemingly simplistic and unceasingly happy celebration of families and weddings turned into the most successful film ever made in India. It was shown to full houses in theatres across the country for months after its release, and there were reports of fans who had watched the film dozens (and some said at least a hundred) of times. There were reports of the theatres being full of families who had emerged, after nearly a decade spent indoors with VCRs, to venture to the theatres to watch a film together. Naturally, they dressed like they were going to a wedding. That is exactly how it felt in the theatres too. It was the one wedding where everyone felt welcome, and perhaps well fed too. Every ceremony featured a lavish feast, which, in keeping with the producers' values, was fully vegetarian. It was as if the age of the 'Maharaja Mac' and other accoutrements of foreign commerce and culture that were all around the screen had not intruded at all. *HAHK* merely evoked an idyllic time when films, and families, were truly 'golden'.

Despite its seeming decision to ignore globalization for the most part, *HAHK* in a sense was India's first popular response to it. Its phenomenon unfolded at a time when the satellite-TV boom had just begun, and everywhere the gyrating bodies of hip-hop and MTV culture marked a new moment in the visual landscape. As a text, *HAHK* may not have been about anything other than its own fantasy, but in the context of the moment in which it was received by its adoring audience, there is much it says about how the audiences were viewing themselves and the world. Some of the participants in my study of its reception, which I conducted in 1995, interpreted the film in a global context even though its predilection was for the most part not (Juluri, 1999). One participant, for example, contrasted the good 'Indian family' system as seen in *HAHK* with what he called the 'contract marriage' system of America. The West, in general, was seen as very family-damaged in that sense, and somehow that was perceived to be the ultimate cause of much that seemed problematic with it. In contrast, India had its traditional, dutiful families, just like what we saw in *HAHK*. As another participant noted,

HAHK was fully in line with the four pursuits of daily life in Hinduism—dharma, artha, kama and moksha—duty, wealth, love and salvation. While *HAHK* did not quite address the afterlife, it did lay out a fairly convincing promise that at least all the other three would ensue logically for its adherents. The story was about everyone doing their duty, and that naturally fit in with the wealth and love and happiness that followed them about.

Since the key ideal of *HAHK* in a sense was that if everyone respected and followed order then all good things would happen, it is worth examining it a little more closely. *HAHK* was closely analysed and criticized by scholars who saw in it everything from Hindutva ideology to gender and class discrimination. Some of these criticisms are indeed relevant. The consumerism in *HAHK* was spectacular, and the opulence of its wedding ceremonies ended up becoming an aspirational criterion for families and wedding planners in real life as well. Its logic about duty and order worked essentially because all the characters stay in their place; there are no inter-class relationships, or 'driver-daughter romances', as one participant in my study said. Unlike many Indian films which were based on exactly those sorts of stories, *HAHK* stayed within certain limits of plausibility, lending itself easily to the interpretation that it was in fact quite realistic for that reason.

But even if *HAHK* troubled critics with its apparent endorsement of the status quo, it did raise the question of what the source of its exuberant delight to audiences was. In one word, it was the family. Even if the film glorified the institution of family in rather unsubtle ways like graffiti on a jeep, the chord it struck with its viewers somehow went deeper. Viewers felt that *HAHK* depicted the way the ideal family ought to be; more precisely, they felt it reminded them of how family life had once been, before modernity and careers and all the rest had led to fragmentations and problems. The family did not figure simply as a fiction for nostalgia either. When viewers spoke of the family, what they were driving at ultimately was a more radical idea about the individual too. One signature phrase that participants in my study used to describe the characters in this film was that they were 'full of sacrifice', that they were ever prepared to sacrifice their own interests for the sake of other members of the family. The sacrificing ideal is by no means uncommon in Indian cinema, and is often criticized by scholars for reinforcing burdens unfairly on certain characters more than others (women, more than men, for example). While this may be a valid criticism in some contexts, perhaps the 'sacrificing nature' viewers saw in *HAHK*—at a time when the main thrust of the cultural climate was towards unabashed self-interest and self-indulgence—was not such a bad thing at all. While I explore this point in some detail in my afterword, suffice it to say for now that *HAHK* brought out a way of looking that seemed completely at odds with the rest of the media and cultural climate of the time. Its utopian promise was that families could live happily and it was a promise that found popular resonance.

For a moment, or three hours, a certain kind of nobility long since absent in Indian popular culture returned with *HAHK*. However, noble thoughts being beholden to the demands of reality—political, economic and such—it was only to be expected that the success of *HAHK* set the example, if not for noble everyday conduct, at least for more commercially successful films to follow, and the expectations of commerce inevitably meant that some of the themes in *HAHK* would turn into abiding formulae in time. The 1995 film *Dilwale Dulhania Le Jayenge* played on the theme of families and marriage, but brought on to the centre stage the figure of the Non-resident Indian as well. The media was already celebrating NRIs for their success, and the film industry acknowledged that the diasporic audience was indeed an important one for it (see R. Dudrah, 2002). From the 1990s, a number of films began to address the lives of Indians abroad, and their return to India too, usually for quests to find spouses and/or fulfil their family duties. The film *Pardes* (1997) was a classic example, and set up Shah Rukh Khan (SRK) as a quintessential hero who is a golden Indian boy despite being successful abroad, and thus a suitable counterfoil to his cousin, who is the corrupted Indian-American and hence not worthy of the lovely Indian village lady he is being set up with. The rise of the diaspora in Indian cinema may have added to the mythology of globalization as India's recognition abroad, although the characters themselves seemed barely rooted in the realities of diasporic experience. For diasporic audiences though, the films offered a sense of authenticity, recollection and recognition of their homeland (C. Brosius, 2005, p. 233). In either context, the films also became about being 'Indian', albeit in ways very different from the older films of the Raj Kapoor or Amitabh Bachchan era. Being Indian was about being a part of a family, but in the lead up to that there had to be a time for friends too, especially for the boyfriends and girlfriends whom young Indians were now talking about.

By the late 1990s, it was evident that globalization started to transform Indian cinema in a number of ways. If MTV and

Channel V had 'discovered' film music as the main source of programming for their vision of a global-Indian youth culture, cinema began to reflect not only the emerging aesthetic conventions of MTV but the broader demographic realities of India as well. One important change took place in the nature of the audience for Hindi cinema. From its early years and until at least the 1980s, Indian cinema had reflected a trans-class (and pan-Indian) sensibility based on its audience. In the 1980s, there were some signs of divergence, with the main viewers of cinema becoming increasingly angry young men of less-privileged-class backgrounds. However, a major change took place with liberalization in the 1990s. The rise of multiplexes and shopping malls in India and the active film-going of diasporic Indian populations ensured that cinema increasingly became a predilection of the privileged. For the first time, even the upper-class, English-educated urban youth, who had earlier viewed domestic cinema as somewhat infra dig, rediscovered their emerging global-Indian identity in Bollywood (as it was now coming to be called as well). It was a sign, perhaps, that globalization was indeed creating classes of people who had more in common across national boundaries than across the compound walls of their own gated communities. Cinema transformed itself in a number of ways because of it, both in form and in content. The films of the late 1990s became slick and less likely to take the sort of technical liberties some of the earlier films did with their rural or mass audiences. In their stories, they held aloft the family as the ideal symbol of morality and the wedding as the ultimate expression of consumer power, but beyond that they forgot all about angry young men and toiling peasants. The new hero of Hindi cinema would instead turn out to be like the American comic book character Archie Andrews. As journalist Manu Joseph (6 November 2000) writes:

> In this new world of Hindi films, pretty pictures with pretty young things, good sound, nifty effects and bouncy soundtracks make a big hit ... [They have] hunky heroes and flirty heroines with attitude togged out in designer labels, airy-fairy sets which look straight out of Friends [and] ear-candy beat driven soundtracks. (p. 1)

The trendsetter in this genre was the 1998 film *Kuch Kuch Hota Hai*. Set in an upscale college campus, it featured its characters playing basketball, sporting fashionable brands and looking rather meticulously like what global marketing executives hoped young people would look like. SRK embodied the aspirations of the emerging young middle-class India by being a good friend, having fun and, despite some emotional and familial difficulties, finally finding good resolution in the happy-family framework. The new hero, as SRK himself put it in an interview, was no longer a vigilante, but a 'yuppie', and as a yuppie he 'promised a better world' (quoted in S. Deshpande, 2005, p. 186). The rise of a yuppie hero was part of a generational phenomenon that marketing researchers had noticed across Asia in the 1990s. Unlike the Western youth cultures of the 1960s and '70s with their protest rock and punk sensibilities, the first experience of youth culture in parts of Asia was emerging in the opposite direction. Youth across Asia were 'rebelling in' to middle-class consumerism, rather than against it (D. McCaughan, 1998). In India, the parents of these young people, who had themselves grown up in the era of Nehruvian austerity, were vicariously enjoying newfound consumer power and spirit through their children (R. Bijapurkar, 1998). The traditional and Nehruvian cultural imperatives to be sensitive about privilege were quickly replaced with a new virtue of unabashed consumerism. In 1998, when a shortage in onions led to a political crisis (see Leela Fernandes, 2006, pp. 198–200), socialites reportedly served onion platters to show they could afford it. In shopping, grooming, travelling and, of course, in weddings, the 1990s saw the rise of affluence and its display on a scale that completely ignored past sensibilities and the present reality that, for most Indians, these things were still beyond reach.

To be fair to the vision of their makers, the 'Riverdale' films of the 1990s did not directly advocate selfish consumerism. They still maintained a great deal of respect for the traditional institutions that were sought to be safeguarded—parents, family and the nation. The characters also seemed like nice people and in some ways seemed more confident than Indian film heroes had ever been. They just dressed better and consumed a lot more, obviously. But, in the drive to make the films more realistic perhaps, some of the sensibilities that made for a pan-Indian, privilege-sensitive set of heroes in the past were lost. Deshpande observes that while the old heroes of Indian cinema were usually vaguely (and therefore uniformly) 'Indian' in their name and characteristics, the new heroes are often specifically constructed as members of particular groups—most often rich, upper-caste Punjabis. Their wealth also marks their behaviour in various ways—a number of recent films feature extensive introductory scenes for the hero which simply involve him being woken up in the morning with a barrage of domestic goods and services. Parents, relatives and servants gather around with bed coffee, CD players and whatever else it takes to rouse the indulgent, if likeable young man, from his dreams and his lavish bedspreads. Many films, like the Hrithik Roshan war film *Lakshya* (2004), also play on the theme of a young man without direction who finally finds his purpose and himself and grows up just right. The formula for growing up in this genre seems to be to achieve something professionally and personally, and to win the recognition of parents, peers and romantic interests. While the striving-for-success stories of these films may resonate with the dreams of young Indians growing up in an age when many have indeed found success and money on a scale beyond those achieved by their parents, there is also an evacuation of many of the realities of Indian everyday life in them. As Deshpande comments, unlike the heroes of the past, the new heroes are presented with little relations outside their class circles. Even the back-up dancers in the increasingly spectacular songs of Indian cinema 'have banished labouring classes' (p. 195). With the splendid exception of *Lagaan* (2001), the peasant has also vanished as a figure in popular cinema. The Indian middle class, much celebrated, is still well under one-fifth of the Indian population; and a realistic estimate of people who could actually afford to live and dress like the characters in these films would be a fraction of even that. The realism of new Indian popular cinema has perhaps come at a price.

The upmarket tastes and lifestyles of the new Indian heroes and heroines are also belied by a populist sense of 'mass' identification that is new as well. The spread of 'Hinglish', supported by the adoption by privileged classes of what were in the past 'mass' practices in cinema, may be creating a false sense of egalitarianism. As Patricia Uberoi (2001) notes, many of the wedding customs depicted in *HAHK* were actually considered 'vulgar', but nonetheless these became common practice, in both North and South India. Heroes, as Deshpande observes, are increasingly measured by their ability to dance—which was once the province of 'extras' and vamps. However, the seeming dissolution of mass and class boundaries in Indian popular culture may be contributing to a false sense of the country's successes and failures. In my study of MTV audiences, I found many participants who interpreted the presence of poor people on TV promos to mean that everyone was doing well under liberalization. With titles like 'V People' and 'Public Demand', music countdowns and vox-pop programmes were spreading a sense of empowerment, which the middle-class youth were accepting quite readily. While a sharp political ideology of the U.S. Republican sort—which holds that when everyone is rich and you are poor it must be your own fault (see S. Jhally & J. Lewis, 1992)—may not exactly be widespread yet in India, the false populism of post-liberalization cinema and TV may be sowing the seeds of such a privatized, socially evacuated sense of one's self.

This is not to suggest that post-Liberalization youth have become superficially 'Westernized' or have grown to dislike their country. On the contrary, they are very nationalistic, and can go so far as to drink tricolour cocktails (in the colour of the Indian flag) at Independence Day parties in the clubs, which the staid Nehruvian would not have dreamt of. The middle-class youth of India are perhaps more strongly, vocally and gesturally 'Indian' than the previous generations; and this pride is often on fierce display at cricket matches as well. Their sense of Indianness also extends to avowed respect for many traditional values, such as taking care of elders, being responsible for their families and so on. But they are also full of what Khilnani (31 January 2005) calls a 'near Promethean self belief that they can do it for themselves'. They may profess family and national values, and enjoy displaying religiousness and tradition in daily life, but they are also aggressive, independent and place a great value of self-advancement and careers (K. Gahlaut, 31 January 2005). Commentators naturally find this phenomenon sadly lacking, and as Khilnani writes, the successful youth of India often 'entertain the illusion that by improving themselves they are aiding their society'. This may be a polite way of saying something quite harsh, which is that, at one level, a society made turgid on media and consumerism and nationalistic propaganda may often be full of individuals who are merely full of themselves.

There are nearly half a billion Indians who were born since Liberalization, when the media boom of a new global era began. They have no direct experience of Gandhi or Nehru's presence on the nation and, at a more immediate level, perhaps their sense of family is also a smaller, fragmented one. Their stories are beginning to be told now, and sometimes we do see the nuances that come from their generational experience—they long for things which were taken for granted in earlier times, even as they express themselves with a confidence that is simply unsurpassed in post-Independence India. Their dreams may be selfish in the short term, but in the long run, they yearn to give back to the country. The number of films that celebrate the returning NRI is only growing. In the low-budget, independent English film *Hyderabad Blues* (1998), Nagesh Kukunoor carefully shows a sense of the returning Hyderabadi-American's cultural dilemmas. He has discovered 'mosh pits' and America, but in India, his relatives still seem to linger in a feudal past compounded by a consumerist present. He stays back for the girl he likes, and in the sequel, the finesse vanishes, but it still shows where India has headed—he runs a call centre; she, a marriage bureau. In bigger films too, the ambitions of service do appear. In *Swades* (2004), Shah Rukh Khan plays a brilliant NASA scientist on a visit to India, who gets pulled into staying back in the village and doing something for it with his engineering skills. The grandest example though of the figure of the successful Indian returning from a diasporic sojourn to help his people is that of *Sivaji* (2007)—the 'Boss' ('B.O.S.S.' is an acronym used in the film's poster and stands for Bachelor of Social Service), played by the great Tamil star Rajinikanth himself. Produced by the venerable South Indian studio AVM and proclaimed as the most expensive film made in India, *Sivaji* released to frenzied adulation in 2007. Indian news channels showed interviews with people who had flown back from the US just to have the pleasure of watching the film in the motherland, although it was widely released in the US as well. In *Sivaji*, Rajinikanth plays a software engineer who returns home to build a medical college that will not take 'donations'. The film spectacularizes his wealth more than anything else. He faces problems with the system. The politicians want bribes, and his competitors cannot let him do anything that will lower their profit margin. Even with all his money, he cannot be generous it seems. So he fights, a bit like an old sacrificing hero and a bit like an Angry Young Man, and finally prevails. Robin Hood, it seems, has to be really, really rich first. One could get used to this sort of model for social redistribution.

Vigilantes, Terrorists, Gangsters

Before the media boom of the 1990s, violence in Indian cinema was by no means inconspicuous, but remained for the most part only as one more part of its 'masala'. Even in films where violence was instrumental—such as the many Angry Young Man hits of the 1970s—there was often a framework of theatricality and even humour within which violence was depicted. As Nandy (1998) writes, the inevitable scenes of violence in Indian cinema were often 'neutralized by comic interludes or by the inclusion of a more comic book version of the violence' (p. 10). The grand climactic fight scenes in smugglers' lairs with which many films ended often had exactly this sort of humour—the hero rescuing the heroine, his mother and innocent captives from the villain with a volley of 'dhishums' (the sound of Hindi film fisticuffs), while his comic sidekick does something ludicrous to an opposite number on the sidelines. The staging of such a fight had hardly any pretence to realism. It was meant to convey just rewards in an almost playful manner, rather than something necessarily vicious or hurtful. The whole fight would pass off quite happily, until the police arrived at the end to wrap it all up and take the bad guys away. But since the 1980s, there has indeed been an increase in the extent, nature and centrality of violence in films. To some extent, this was brought about by the rise of new, stylized directors who brought a gritty realism to violence that made even the best action films of the past seem amusing. For example, director Ram Gopal Verma's Telugu hit Shiva (1989) broke new ground in portraying violence as something real, dark and dangerous. It was an Angry Young Man film in the sense that the hero was a college student, but it unfolded without the pretence of entertainment or levity. In contrast, in films with iconic megastars like Amitabh Bachchan, Rajinikanth or Chiranjeevi, violence was often only a tool to symbolize the supreme potency of the hero—his fists crackled with electricity and caused the villains to fly out in ever-widening distances. However, with films like *Shiva*, cinema was acknowledging that violence was not merely meant to be seen as a story any more, but as a representation of reality.

In the years that followed, not only did violence become more graphic in films but the lives of those engaged in violence as a career (or calling) caught the attention of Indian cinema in numerous ways. The last decade saw the rise of gangster films (*Satya*, *Company*); films about terrorism, war and Hindu--Muslim conflict (*Roja*, *Bombay*, *Mission Kashmir*); films that celebrated vigilantism as a form of social justice (*Indian*, *Aparachitudu*) and films that celebrated militant action for revolution or even social change (*Rang De Basanti*, *The Rising*). There were also a number of films which featured violently psychopathological individuals (*Darr*) and even bordered on horror. All of these examples raise one fundamental question—What is the overall message that we find in recent cinema about violence?

In the films of one director, at least, violence came to be elevated to the level of social commentary, political critique and even personal philosophy. For Shankar, nothing seems to ail India more than corruption, and nothing will help to get rid of it but swift and vigilante-style violence. His 1996 film *Bharateeyudu* (made in Tamil, Telugu and Hindi) features the versatile Kamal Haasan (who has since shown his own penchant for films about violent psychopaths) and tells the story of Senapati, an elderly Indian freedom fighter who

comes out of retirement to slay corrupt government officials
and get India back on track. *Bharateeyudu* reimagines India
from the perspective of non-non-violence, so to speak. It
begins with a portrait of a country marked by apathy, lethargy
and rampant corruption. The cause of such corruption, it is
implied, is that India followed the wrong leaders all along.
Only a militant hero, it says, can set things right. Gandhi and
Nehru are marginalized in the film's reinterpretation of India's
freedom movement, and instead, Subhas Chandra Bose is
rediscovered as a suitably militaristic and patriotic freedom
fighter. Senapati, we learn through his flashbacks, was a
militant freedom fighter, and even joined Bose's Indian
National Army to fight the British during World War II. He
is forced to turn from his quiet life as an elderly parent into
that of a violent avenger because a corrupt doctor refuses to
treat his daughter unless he is paid a bribe. Senapati henceforth
proceeds to execute the corrupt everywhere, and makes sure
to record his executions and broadcast them on satellite TV
as well. The spectacle of lethal punishment instils immediate
order in the country. Everything begins to work properly
and, even as a police dragnet closes in, Senapati renders one
last act of justice—executing his own son for corruption.
Then, he escapes, and makes a call to warn India that he is
watching, presumably from Singapore, a place often
mentioned in the film as an example of strict rules leading to
good government and prosperity for the people.

Coming as this film did in the early years of Liberalization,
it echoed a growing sense of middle-class impatience with
the government. Equally, the film also seemed to speak in a
new visual language closer to the tastes of the growing middle-
class audience rather than those of the 'mass' audience. As

T. Niranjana and S.V. Srinivas (1996) note, 'each one of Senapati's killings is graphically depicted, but there is a striking economy of violence in his actions ... (his) murders are quickly and efficiently performed—deft use of his fingers and a couple of thrusts of his knife is all a killing takes' (p. 3131). In contrast, Senapati's son (also portrayed by Kamal Haasan) is shown in regular, lengthy, film-style fights. In a few years, as if neither form of cinematic violence would suffice, Shankar's *Aparachitudu* (2005; *Anniyan* in Tamil) would move into the terrain of mythology-inspired torture, still functioning under a similar logic of vigilante justice against corruption. The hero, a gentle, honest, law-abiding small-time lawyer from a family of Brahmin priests, turns into a violent super-avenger who can be reached on his own website, naturally. People email him complaints about officials who won't do their jobs, and he sets off at night to slay them according to the bizarre methods described in an ancient text about what kinds of punishments await sinners in the afterlife. A caterer providing unhygienic food to railway passengers is boiled in oil. A man who refuses to share his car with an accident victim has a herd of stampeding buffaloes let loose on him. Once word about Aparachitudu gets around, Indian traffic improves miraculously, with everyone starting to drive in their own lanes, and order and efficiency come to prevail at last. In the end, though, it is not politics but psychotherapy that prevails in the film.

In some ways, celebrating punitive violence against a generic foe called 'corruption' was an appealing narrative option, but one that had little real-life resonance compared to the other sort of violence many films began to engage with in the decade. The 1990s were not only a decade of economic growth and media proliferation in India, but also of numerous egregious acts of violence, from riots to terrorism and bomb-attacks on civilians. Terrorism was not an unknown concern in popular Indian cinema, although one of its first references was largely humorous. In the 1987 hit *Mr India*, we see references to the 'foreign hand' that we were told those days caused a lot of bad things to happen in India. The arch-villain of *Mr India*, Mogambo, is of indeterminate nationality but harbours only one intention—to destroy India. Mogambo—may he be pleased—was one of India's most popular villains and, despite causing much grief, was closer in his mannerisms to the ludicrous villain Goldmember in the *Austin Powers* films rather than any real-life terrorist masterminds. By the 1990s though, Hindu–Muslim riots and India–Pakistan conflicts both became more serious concerns, and the films turned to them in some earnestness as well.

The 1992 film *Roja* addresses the question of Kashmiri insurgency, but starts its story in a village at the opposite end of India. The protagonist is kidnapped while serving in Kashmir, and the film shows the efforts of his wife—a Tamil villager who cannot even speak Hindi—to deal with the government and get his release. At the same time, a relationship of sorts forms between the hero and his captor, and dialogues like 'Is it in your religion that man should kill man?' (quoted in N. Dirks, 2001) suggest an attempt less to 'understand' militancy perhaps, but to reassure the audience that the problem is not with religion—as many had come to believe—but with those who manipulate it for political reasons. However, it is not merely a religious misunderstanding that is sought to be cleared but a nationalist one too. In many ways, the hero counters his opponent's arguments about jihad not with religious ideas but simply with the idea of India. A highlight of the film—which reportedly led to ecstatic audience reactions—was the hero's attempt to shield with his own body an Indian flag that has been set on fire by his captors. On a happier note though, *Roja* also brought to fame the man who would make India's best music of the decade—the composer A.R. Rahman.

The most well-known and perhaps controversial film on the subject of Hindu-Muslim relations in a time of increasing hostility and violence was Mani Ratnam's *Bombay* (1995). A Hindu man and a Muslim woman fall in love and escape their small-town families to start a new life in Bombay (again with excellent music from Rahman). The divisive politics of the Ram-temple movement and the riots that followed catch up with the couple, even as they have twin children who presumably symbolize that there is enough in India to accommodate the desires of both Hindus and Muslims (R. Vasudevan, 2001). *Bombay* broke a long-standing taboo in Indian cinema about inter-religion romance between characters, and the subtle power play involved in choosing a Hindu man and a Muslim woman rather than the other way around was analysed closely. On the other hand, other films of the time continued to make moral points about Hindu–Muslim unity rather more plainly. Heroes could admonish feuding Hindus and Muslims by pounding their hands with a rock and showing them that their blood was the same colour. It was not as lofty as *Amar Akbar Anthony* giving blood to their mother in another era, but the point had indeed been made.

Hindu–Muslim brotherhood was perhaps not too difficult an ideal for cinema to extol, but then it frequently had to be done in the context of a larger geopolitical shadow, that of the question of Pakistan and its support to terrorism against India. Sometimes this was done crudely, by positing characters like 'good Indian Muslims' against the 'bad Pakistani terrorists'. In the 2002 Telugu film *Khadgam* (Dagger), for example, a Hyderabadi Muslim auto driver is one of the main characters, and saves a bus full of Hindu pilgrims from being attacked by a Muslim mob. Later, he protects his brother—a Pakistan-trained terrorist—from the police, accusing them of harassing Muslims, but in the end, he disowns the brother. The film is naturally full of symbolism about Hindu-Muslim harmony and takes some time to condemn Osama Bin Laden and General Musharraf (and, interestingly enough, the World Bank as well).

Many films may have advocated such messages with varying degrees of conviction or credibility, but perhaps the most compelling terrorist film of the period was *Mission Kashmir* (2000). *Mission Kashmir* was aimed as a 'crossover' film, and combined the taut suspense and drama of a political thriller with the drama of a family conflict. The story takes place in Kashmir at the height of the militancy and focuses on the tension between a Kashmiri Muslim police officer, his Hindu wife and their adopted son who becomes a militant under the tutelage of a shadowy Afghan mastermind. The harsh twist that runs through the characters is that it is the police officer who inadvertently kills the little boy's parents in a raid before he adopts him. Altaf (played by Hrithik Roshan) has two things on his mind—jihad, and revenge against his foster father. The only things that stop him, naturally, are the budding romance with his childhood sweetheart and his enduring affection for his adoptive Hindu mother. Talk of jihad, fatwas and Mujahideen run through the film, as does a strong sense of longing for the loss of paradise. In the end, Altaf has to choose between his desire to kill his foster father to avenge his parents and his love for his foster mother and all that is decent in the world, and turn against his mercenary mentor and save the subcontinent from holocaust. It is about recognizing himself, finally, as someone who is defined by love (of a mother and a girlfriend) rather than by anger or jihadi ideology. It is about saving the world too, like any good Hollywood thriller, but in this the hero saves the world for mom. The moral of *Mission Kashmir*, if one may be proposed, is that the moral and emotional obligations that we have towards each other in our relationships call on us to overcome any perceived divisions of religion, race or nationality. It is about universalism, and while there is indeed plenty of violence in the film, the message is that at some point the inexorable cyclicality of violence must be stopped. That is how it all happened in the first place—revenge bred revenge. Someone had to stop it, and rise above the anger. *Mission Kashmir* ends with a song of hope and new beginnings.

If violence, or at least militancy, was downplayed in the context of terrorism and Hindu–Muslim conflict in some stories, there was one growing genre in which violence was indeed the professional raison d'être of the genre itself—the gangster film. Beginning with *Parinda* in the late 1980s, a number of films came to be made about the Bombay underworld, often leading to comments about how the film industry was cuddling up to its not-so-nice underworld financiers. In *Satya* (1998), we see the old story of a small-town boy coming to Bombay to make it big retold in the gripping form of a gangster saga. In *Company* (2000), we see shades of *Scarface*, but its whole thrust seems to be towards depicting its characters not as mindless professional killers but essentially as people with families and friends, going about doing their business while occasionally running up against moral dilemmas.

In some ways, films like *Company* showed globalization at its rawest. The world in these films was not merely one of happy foreign locations for heroes named Raj or Prem. It was a place of seedy characters and seedier deals. It spanned both the slums of Mumbai and the high-rise skylines of Hong Kong and Dubai, showing how life and death and everything in between unfolded over telephones. It included small-town-boys-turned-hitmen, as well as captains of commerce and pillars of politics, in its wake. As a line from the catchy theme song of *Company*, 'Gandha Hain', states, it was a world exemplified by the 'dhoti pe coat' and the 'dil mein chot'. The gangs, it seems, are not above feeling either the cultural contradictions of a changing world or the pain and loss of life in their line of work. They are outside law and morality, but only so far, according to the films of their pantheon. They love their families and God. They sing too, and in the case of one exceptional thug, they are even visited by the spirit of Mahatma Gandhi, who reassures us, as recently as 2006, that he has never really left India.

'Global and Medieval', but Gandhian Still?

The best way perhaps to evaluate what all the violence in the media means to India today is by turning to Indian cinema's one incredible, box-office storming paean to non-violence. *Lage Raho Munna Bhai* (2006) was the sequel to *Munna Bhai M.B.B.S* (2003), a comedy about a small-time gangster who strong-arms and smooth-talks his way through medical school to prove himself to his father, and ends up healing patients and cold-hearted technocratic doctors alike. In the sequel, he starts off by pretending to be a professor of Gandhian studies to impress a lady conducting a radio quiz about Gandhi, but ends up with the Mahatma's apparition by his side (as his loyal side-kick Circuit remains on the other). Following the Mahatma's gentle admonitions, Munna Bhai wins over everyone without recourse to his usual gangster techniques, and along the way provides Gandhian solutions for troubled callers on a radio show as well. The film became wildly popular and led to a widespread use of ideas from it to deal with day-to-day situations—students gave out flowers as a form of protest, exasperated citizens learnt to embarrass obstinate officials rather than fight with them. The practice was called 'Gandhigiri' (a pun on 'dadagiri' or gangsterism), and its effects even reached the one place the Mahatma might have thought needed it (albeit for a different reason)—in the summer of 2007, anxious green-card applicants sent 'get well soon' flowers, following the film, to the office of the U.S. Department of Homeland Security.

The popularity of the *Munna Bhai* films reminds us of the enduring significance of Mahatma Gandhi as a figure in India, even if what he signifies to different groups is frequently quite different from the nuances of his own thought. As an important figure in the public imagination, the meaning of Gandhi in post-globalization India is caught up in a number of political forces, as Shanti Kumar (2006) shows in his study. Although the Left, Right and caste-based parties may all prefer to marginalize Gandhi's status as the pre-eminent 'Father' of independent India, his hallowed status suggests that for many people, he is someone who must be accorded absolute reverence. Caricaturing Gandhi in a mean-spirited way, as the American grunting men's magazine *Maxim* once did, is generally not tolerated. Perhaps, for the middle-class youth, Gandhi (like 'India' or 'Ram') is seen as someone to be respected, even if not necessarily as someone to be emulated for how he lived, or even how he thought about the world.

In such a context, would the popular resonance of *Lage Raho Munna Bhai* and the rise of 'Gandhigiri' suggest that there is something different about how this film constructed Gandhian philosophy? There was at least one important difference between the Gandhi of *Munna Bhai* and other cinematic depictions. Although Gandhi has in recent years been depicted in a number of ways in cinema, ranging from a portrait of a leader as a young man (Shyam Benegal's *The Making of the Mahatma*, 1996) to that of a troubled father (*Gandhi, My Father*, 2007), he has more often been invoked as a conscience-figure (the more plaintive and imaginative of these being *Maine Gandhi Ko Nahin Mara*, 2005). However, the use of Gandhi as the nation's 'eternal witness' reduces his depiction to a sorry, helpless figure in some cases. In 2005, a Telugu play being staged in Hyderabad, *Baapu Cheppina Maata* (What Bapu told us), set Gandhi up eloquently as a witness to the daily depravities of the economically booming India. Corrupt officials and land-grabbing real-estate sharks collude right under his statue to take over public land. The statue awakens, and brings some admonitions in its wake that, on the whole, serve to make everyone involved feel very bad about their actions. The invocation of Gandhi in this sense continues the practice of thinking of him reverentially and of how upset he must be by the way things are in his country today, but capitulates to the pathos at that point. However, in *Lage Raho Munna Bhai*, Gandhi had the advantage of having a very large gentleman on his payroll. He did not seem a helpless figure at all and merely injected his perennial wisdom into the idiom of the affable street thug, who is in many ways the everyman of Indian cinema today.

In an age when cynicism and force seem like requirements for daily life, *Lage Raho Munna Bhai*'s Gandhi seemed to revive truth and non-violence as worthy ideals. The immense success of the film raises the question of not only what Indians see in Gandhi today, but also how relevant the ideal of ahimsa is today. To begin with, we can look a little more closely at what *Munna Bhai* seems to say about these ideals. Despite its apparent revival of Gandhian ideals in a newfound idiom, *Lage Raho Munna Bhai*'s engagement with certain important elements of Gandhian thought seem not to differ very much with the broader consensus on these matters in India today. For instance, Munna Bhai's idea of non-violence is embodied, inevitably, in an instance of turning the other cheek (unsuccessfully for the cause, because when he is slapped a second time, he throws his restraint out and beats up the man who dared slap him twice). In general, Munna Bhai's tactics are anything but Gandhian in the strict sense—for example, he holds an obnoxious yuppie upside down over a ledge to make him remember his filial responsibilities and attend his father's birthday party. Gandhi himself sometimes appears to express simplified homilies about his own self, admonishing Munna to speak the truth and tell all to his lady friend, for example. In some ways, *Lage Raho Munna Bhai* appears to understand Gandhi and his principles exactly the same way India does in a popular sense today. Yet, both

Munna Bhai and India are more immersed in some ways of thinking that are closer to Gandhi than even they are aware of. That, I believe, is the single remaining line of hope for the world in India today.

One widespread limitation these days in thinking about ideals like ahimsa is the belief that non-violence is nothing more than refusing to retaliate when someone hits you—a common myth which the Jesuit scholar of non-violence Simon Harak (2000) aptly compares to defining marriage as not sleeping with anyone but your spouse! Understood in this narrow way, non-violence is often seen, especially in these days of widely felt concerns about terrorism, as irrelevant and even potentially harmful, encouraging passivity instead of determined action. To those observers, especially from abroad, who visit India with the romantic expectation that the land of Gandhi would be full of non-violence in a literal sense, the reality is shocking, sometimes leading through a sort of backlash to even more unrealistic judgements about Indians being somehow more violent than they really may be! Even an astute Indian observer of India like Varma (2004), for example, writes that:

> Indians are not non-violent per se. The myth of ahimsa or non-violence, as an intrinsic part of the Indian personality, was sold by Mahatma Gandhi and conveniently bought by the nation . . . Indians are capable of a great degree of violence.
> (p. 165)

Is ahimsa merely a 'myth'? Did the Mahatma do nothing more than peddle us towards freedom on the strength of a euphemism? Our limited understanding of non-violence and our seemingly endless litany of examples of real-life violence both would suggest that there is some basis to such a cynical view. Varma himself lists about two pages of examples of violence committed by Indians in his book, ranging from the abuse of domestic servants to the 'violence meted out to animals in vegetarian India' (p. 166). Since globalization, it even appears that there has been an increase in certain kinds of violence, or at least in the media's coverage of it. Certain forms of violence are often attributed to the social and economic consequences of globalization, with rising poverty, desperation and frustration driving some young men to everything from crime to political violence. Henry Luce's (2007) phrase 'global and medieval' captures some realities and inequalities in post-globalization India aptly. After all, even in a poster case for liberalization like the city of Hyderabad, where a booming Information-Technology and real-estate business has led many to revel in unheard-of levels of wealth, poverty in the surrounding regions has engendered farmer suicides and an ongoing Maoist struggle. However, contrasting the 'global' of programmers, nightclubs and multinational companies against the 'medieval' of poverty and lack of basic resources like water is, however, only one part of the picture. There has simultaneously been a co-optation between the global and the medieval in India. Recent years have also seen the rise of wealthy and powerful people who lack Enlightenment liberality and even traditional Indian humanity. They are the sort often highlighted in 'dowry harassment' cases, even as they might not hesitate sometimes to abuse the dowry laws if that was more profitable for them. They are the ugly side of India shining and rising. In some ways, globalization seems to have complicated the question of violence, making it come now from many directions, local and global, the slum and the mansion.

The realities of the existence of violence in various forms notwithstanding, the core issue that *Lage Raho Munna Bhai*'s revival of Gandhian ideals makes us think about is not so much whether Indians are literally non-violent, but really, of *how, and with what consequences, we think about violence in general.* Non-violence, after all, is not merely a simple code of behaviour forbidding retaliation, nor even a protest technique (as many in the West think it is); but really a philosophy, a way of thinking about the world. In the ahimsa religions of Jainism, Buddhism and Hinduism, in the lives of numerous saints and reformers, in Mahatma Gandhi and sometimes even in our single biggest cultural mirror for our own selves in the modern era—our films—the philosophy of ahimsa has remained; if not in impeccable practice, at least in our assumptions about the world. Indian common sense, I often presume to believe, embodies ahimsa much more than what passes for common sense about violence and human nature in the age of global media discourses today. American films and TV, for example, seem to view violence as natural, eternal and, these days, even more inevitable because of the 'clash of civilizations'. Indian cinema may depict violence—lots of it; but in the end, it asserts an idealism closer to that of Gandhi than of either social Darwinists or the 'clash of civilizations' theorist Samuel Huntington (1993). Even if Hindus and Muslims attack each other in our films, it is not because they are Hindus and Muslims, and not in the least because of Hinduism and Islam. Even if violence is the chosen career or calling of characters in our films, it is not the core of their selves, which is still defined by who they are as brothers or sons or fathers. Even if it takes the character of a 'goonda' who is intellectually and morally incapable of being Gandhian, we still find that there is something in the return of Gandhi that speaks to us today.

The 'myth' then is perhaps not that we are 'non-violent', but the opposite. As Varma himself notes later in his book, despite all the reprehensible examples of Indian violence he lists, India is still less inclined towards violence as a solution in general. There are no instances of Indian aggression against foreign countries. As he puts it, 'Indians are not inclined towards self-annihilation' (p. 166) and would rather compromise—give the Mughals and the British their political power, for example, as long as they could keep their gods and their religion. He also draws on recent studies of Hindu-Muslim violence in India to argue that in spite of the alarm that such violence has provoked, seen in the context of one billion people, and over a span of fifty-odd years since Independence, Hindus and Muslims have indeed for the most part lived together peacefully. All of this, he says, is once again not because Indians are intrinsically non-violent, but are just 'being practical in understanding the limits of violence' (p. 8). Such a practicality may come from the knowledge that violence is wasteful, a distraction from the pursuit of life and Lakshmi. But like many other things in India, it may be the case that this seemingly easy-going indifference, which results in the avoidance of violence wherever possible, has deeper cultural and philosophical roots than may be apparent. It is perhaps those very roots that still move us today in films like *Lage Raho Munna Bhai*, even if many who make or watch these films are not explicitly aware of it. A way of understanding the world based on the basic premise of not harming anyone or anything is India's greatest cultural and spiritual resource. Even in the age of globalization and global violence.

It may be instructive that the age of globalization in India began with an ultraviolent film like *Bharateeyudu* which essentially rejected Gandhi and proposed stern and violent action as a solution for all of India's problems, but came back, even in its most un-Gandhian genre, to something important that it felt Gandhi stood for. Even if the young assertive middle-class can-doers of globalizing India hold essentially two opposite views—of Gandhi as an icon on one hand, and ahimsa as an irrelevant fad on the other—there is something in them that allows them to see films like *Lage Raho Munna Bhai* as appealing and even inspiring. It is that 'something' that I turn to in my afterword. I call it 'Life', somewhat loosely, and what I believe it encompasses is a way of knowing the world that is always slightly beyond the scope of modernity and its way of knowing. It is the ground on which Gandhi stood in his critique of violence and modernity, and it is not unlike the ground which a small part of being Indian (at least in the cinema hall) still draws upon for meaning and experience. The Mahatma may not have liked movies, but it is in cinema perhaps that his spirit has remained more than in India's politics or economics.

AFTERWORD

LIFE

Om Shanti Om
Anukokunda Oka Roju
Peepli (Live)
Harishchandrachi Factory

FREMONT, CALIFORNIA'S 'NAZ CINEMA' AS IT WAS CALLED UNTIL recently, is where many of us in the San Francisco Bay Area go to watch our Indian films, even in the age of instant DVDs and downloads. It feels like a small piece of home tucked into an anyplace-USA sort of shopping plaza, with a restaurant next door that serves even that rarest of delights—Indian–Chinese food. In an age when film-going in India seems more American than in the US, there is a sort of charm in the seemingly unchanging world of Naz Cinema. (Of course, what it has finally changed to is rather Indian too, it's now Big Cinema, a property of the Reliance ADA Group.) I have marked the last few years of my life with memorable films here. *Kaante* (2002)—the singing *Reservoir Dogs* as my students called it—was the first. I remember it well because I nearly left halfway through. The usher asked me, incredulously, 'It seems it has been a long time since you watched a Hindi film.' I said yes, for I had only recently moved to the Bay Area with its Indian theatres and culture, after many years in small American towns with no Indian films. I was so off the grid I had obviously forgotten the most elementary part of the Indian cinema experience. The usher shouted, 'Interval!' Then, I understood—first with embarrassment, then with the relief that it was not over yet, neither the film nor something I knew of myself and my world. In a few years, there would be time for *our* first film together, for my wife and me; and later, our first *Telugu* film

together, in a theatre, in America. It all seemed so new and
exciting at first. These were followed by other landmarks.
Our first good film together, for a change, was a film about
children—*Taare Zameen Par* (2007). Then Indian–Chinese,
relatives, groceries, the usual things. Nothing much changed
in and around the theatre, except its name, and the one
nearby bookstore that closed. But in time, the changes came—
the changes we wanted. Our family grew. Our son was born.
We knew he was coming—perhaps by a coincidence worthy
of my lifelong debt to Indian cinema—not too far from Naz
Cinema, in the hospital next door.

It is not too much of a leap perhaps then that I should
choose a suburban American mall with an Indian theatre as
the setting for the meaning-of-life chapter in this book. In
and around Naz Cinema, over the years, on dull Sunday
afternoons full of thoughts for the week's classes ahead, I
convinced myself often that the place really told me all that
was important for appreciating Indian cinema's place in our
modern, global lives today. Modernity was everywhere, at its
best and its worst, as I stood gazing from that sprawling,
mostly empty parking lot outside Naz Cinema. On one side
of the building which houses the theatre, amidst a row of
small shops, there is a recruitment centre for the US military.
This was the time after 9/11 and Iraq, and the posters there
seemed to me like a portal for young people to get sucked
into a world of violence and pain with little justification. A
little distance away, on the edge of the parking lot, there is a
hospital, where lives were being saved, and new lives being
welcomed into this world. It was one afternoon, right there,
that I finally thought I saw the big picture about Indian
cinema. In between these two places lay—bare like a grid—

the land that was perhaps once farm or forest, and was now marked by rows of well-marked parking spaces, just like the slots we will occupy all our lives, from hospital nurseries to schools to offices to perhaps retirement homes. Yet, it is on this ground, between the triumphs and terrors of reason and modernity that we find—in our films, in our own lives—something called Life.

Some of the nicer ideals of modernity are obvious—equality, freedom, democracy. But when we consider everything else, it is not surprising that some of our most profound thinkers, like Mahatma Gandhi, and even our most popular entertainments, our films, reject modernity in some important ways. Modernity is based on a way of knowing that presupposes great control, precision, detachment from feeling. It has given us mastery, nothing less than that, over almost everything, even life itself. But the cost of such a way of knowing is that it comes with great arrogance, indifference, cruelty even. Modernity has fundamentally reversed many aspects of our ways of living and knowing. We live now for our own selves and not for others; with self-interest and indeed, selfishness, becoming enshrined as the founding principle of our economies and our social philosophies. We live now in a world that is based on calculations of control and risk and not on trust. We live in a world where rules create more of a stifling absurdity rather than justice and order. We live now, most of all, in a world where 'sentiments' are seen as having no place in our understanding of things, leading to a point where even extreme, inexcusable and unnatural cruelty has become normalized. Bhikhu Parekh's (2001) summary of Gandhi's view of modernity may be relevant here:

In Gandhi's view modern civilization rested on and was
sustained by massive violence ... against oneself [in the
form of a society filled with] ambitious, competitive, and
mutually fearful persons ... [and] also ... against other
persons at both the personal and collective levels ... In
Gandhi's view violence 'oozed from every pore' of modern
society, and had so much become a way of life that *human
beings today were in danger of losing the capacity to notice its
pervasive presence.* (p. 83, emphasis added)

In the age of the global media, with its copycat 'reality shows'
that feed on insects and insults and intrigues and injuries, its
news programmes which circle around tragedies like
cormorants on the wings of cameras and clichés, its
advertisements that promise the impossible, it would seem
that we have few resources left in our culture to feel the truth,
let alone understand it. We are indeed 'in danger of losing
the capacity to notice (the) pervasive presence' of violence in
the world today; whether it is the violence that exists against
nature, animals and every form of life that is being destroyed
or devoured every single day; the violence in the form of
political and economic decisions that have created famine,
displacement, farmer suicides and all-around poverty; or the
violence that has seeped into our most intimate relationships,
turning us into hardened individuals incapable of harmony
with ourselves or with others. Even the forms of violence that
we do notice—or the media notice for us—such as wars,
terrorism and crime, we rarely see as part of the bigger
picture, beset as we are with bits of soundbites and clichés
from the received wisdom of the Left and the Right. We are,
in some ways, on the brink of oblivion and obliviousness as a
planet (indeed that is perhaps why the West is at its best

when it makes doomsday films, whether the thoughtful but dark *Children of Men*, or the annoying but too-true satire *Idiocracy*). There are enough reasons for gloom and doom in the media environment in India too—the necromania of some news channels comes once again to mind—but somehow, there are moments in our films that belie that. The story of our films—the story in our films, to be more accurate—has told us of a better way. It has not been perfect, for the storytellers and the stars themselves are part of a real, imperfect world, driven by desire and ego and fear. But the story in Indian cinema, on the whole, has come closer to a story of who we are than anything else our media or arts have produced in the last century. In a world of broken mirrors, it is as expansive, and unsullied a cultural reflection as we might find of ourselves and measure ourselves against. Indian cinema is our dream world, but that does not make it any less real, meaningful or important. There is a difference. Our dreams are where we go to be happy people, period. Our films tell us we can be good and happy people, even if the idea of 'good' has stretched extensively over the decades to include thugs and gangsters too. A hundred years ago, it all began in the shadow of one man whose relevance to our ideals, if not our reality, has been barely appreciated. It seems to have returned, so to speak, like a ghost, like a 'chemical luccha', with him. What has changed, from Gandhi to Gandhigiri? What has stayed the same? Where do our films, and our lives, go from here? What happens after the film ends and we leave the suburban parking lot?

Since 1991, India's real life and India's story about itself have both acquired one feature—confidence. Whether this is misplaced, or whether it is even desirable in the light of the obvious disparities with which our economic success has played out, the fact remains that confidence is indeed our reigning cultural feature in some ways now. India and its popular cinema have journeyed together down a momentous century, from colony to emerging power. Now, as India and its films confront the future from a moment of high globalization, it may seem that the twenty-first century will be India's, as some observers have proclaimed. But we must also ask, as the saying goes, whether 'India will win the world but lose its soul'? Our films, like us, are perhaps struggling to avoid this choice. Like us, our films have gained from the benefits of modernity. Since globalization, there is no doubt that we are more confident, wealthier as a whole, taking on challenges and opportunities around the world. Some of our recent films, like *Om Shanti Om* (2007), seem to have been made to show nothing more than the fact that we can afford to put on a show! Our films have reached a point of opulence and craftsmanship where they can turn on their own history to make 'retro' stories. Our success with modernity, though, is seen not merely in lavish chandelier-centred spectacles about retro and reincarnation. We have also seen the rise of smaller, offbeat and sometimes exceptionally intriguing films which capture the strangeness of everyday life in a time unlike anything our parents or grandparents knew. For me, the Telugu suspense thriller *Anukokunda Oka Roju* (Unexpectedly one day, 2005) will remain the definitive story of globalization, not just because of its haunted exploration of my hometown, Hyderabad, but also because of its depiction of contemporary everyday Indian middle-class life.

The story of this film is simple yet twisted. The heroine goes to a party where she is given a 'date rape' drug. She wakes up in her own bed the next day and discovers it is actually the day after, she has no memory of what has happened in the period in between. Then, she finds, people are trying to kill her. With its vivid images of rich young men and women with their parties and SUVs cruising the night streets of Hyderabad, and the more modest lives of middle-class youth with their ambitions weaving in and out, the story heads to a frightening and utterly bizarre climax. In the end, one of the characters comments nonchalantly, 'Can it really be true that so many madmen are roaming freely in the city?' An apt comment on the urban anomie that has become a reality in what were once laid-back small towns. What makes this such a contemporary globalization story, though, is not just the SUVs and parties and lunatics roaming freely in the cities. Just as in India's real-life story, what triumphs in this story is not the force of fists but just quick thinking, using one's own wits. If there is one survival principle in India today, it is improvisation. There are no rules and no grand social visions any more. It is all about 'just adjust'. In our politics and in our daily lives, it's what we have, and it seems to work. But the bigger question, of course, is how much will this guide us into the twenty-first century that has been promised to us? What will be left of us, our land and air and trees (and rocks too, in the case of Hyderabad; the Queen of the Deccan has been robbed of her most astounding jewels)? What will be the value of our lives in a world where everything has been stretched taut by contradiction and inequality? Can we tell a story that lives up to the concerns of our times? In a world with too many stories (or bits and pieces of them), thanks to the media, can we even tell a decent story?

It is perhaps no surprise that two of the most unusual and

yet memorable films in these years so close to the centennial of *Raja Harischandra* deal with the question of how to tell a story about the world, even if in very different ways. *Peepli (Live)* (2010) disturbs our story—our complacence in our new post-liberalization selves. If we have too easily accepted the shallow explanation that our new prosperity and pride have come naturally and at no cost, *Peepli (Live)* shows us the contrary. It shows a story of destructiveness, greed, cynicism and absurdity. It is the story for the media age. We all know only too well know what happens when the boy falls into a well in India. *Peepli (Live)* savages the media-feeding frenzy, but it also shows what really has happened—what we don't think about even when we have learned, perforce, to think critically about the wastefulness and, on occasion, the viciousness of the media. Its image of an elderly man digging what turns out to be his own grave—a sideline to the circus, as it were—haunts us in the end, as does its simple evocation of cause and effect at the end—the rising cities and the ruined villages. *Peepli (Live)* marks the entry—a powerful one—of what we used to teach in the confines of our critical media-studies classrooms, into the popular consciousness. But just like the critical curriculum—and unlike our usual cinema—it leaves us with no answers, or anything resembling a sense of closure. For a moment, we feel like the bewildered, battered little human being at the end, confronted by a world of altitude and concrete and no meaning, no way home again.

I remain though, like our films, a fan of the happy ending. If *Peepli (Live)* represents what—to many of us of a certain educational and cultural disposition—feels like the end of all our theorizing, then *Harishchandrachi Factory* (2009), a film about the making of India's first film, feels like the opposite, like an 'art' film that has the effect of a cheerful, entertaining 'masala' film. *Harishchandrachi Factory* could have been a dry documentary about the man who is revered as the father of the Indian film industry. But it chooses to become something else—almost a textbook example of the 'light-hearted romp' it has been characterized as. It misses, as critics have noted, the chance to dramatize the conflicts of the period, the colonial and racial issues, the caste issues and so on. It almost seems like a children's play from school, a happy, easy, ever-moving breeze that starts with a magic show and ends with the greatest magic trick performed in Hindustan—its first ever film. The fascinating thing about this particular way of telling the story is that, despite its apparent naiveté, it is actually making a point for our times. There is no conflict, and mysteriously, for the time and for a man who made films about the gods, there is no religion either in his life, it seems. He is a happy man, and a good man. So is everyone else. Almost everyone in this film—Phalke, his wife, his children, his British colleagues—are nice to each other, and happy for it. The dawn of Indian cinema is almost incidental. But its cheerfulness does seem apt and prophetic. *Harishchandrachi Factory*, like Indian cinema, is after all, about what lay audiences would call 'sentiments'.

In the century that has spanned from *Raja Harischandra* to *Harishchandrachi Factory*, our films, and our lives, have seen changes that cannot be easily summarized. Throughout it all, even as everything changed, the ideal of sentiments, of feeling something in the stories of our lives, has remained important to how we perceive them. Sentiments alone may not be sufficient to provide a grand social or political vision that can guide the nation and the world—although the evidence of the Mahatma's life and legacy suggests we can't rule out the possibility this may have happened in the past—but they are one of the best things we have going for us in the world today. Even if the demands of politics and business have marginalized it from real life, at least in our films, in the dark stillness of our theatres and our inner selves, we still feel it. In fact, if there is one thing that Indian cinema has had in common throughout the decades, it is precisely that it has been about feeling. We felt Tyagayya and Tukaram's devotion to God in their songs. We felt Raj Kapoor's desperation when hiding from a hypocritical mob. We felt Amitabh Bachchan's righteous anger. And, in an age when too much feeling is not considered all that cool in an MTV sort of way, we felt Munna Bhai's discovery of Bapu, without taking tension at it. In all these cases, though, what was important was the fact that these films did not simply make us feel something for the mere sake of melodramatic titillation as concocted by producers' formulae (sometimes, granted) but also *made us feel strongly about what the right thing was*. Our emotional experiences, in other words, were also our ethical touchstones. It is easy to assume that these ethical touchstones were part of some unchanging ancient morality, or to denigrate them as mere ideological conspiracies of a capitalist media system. But the best way to approach the 'right thing' that our films have sought to present for our sensibilities over the years is by contrasting them with what the rest of our culture, and our times, seem to be saying about how the world works.

We now live in a media environment in which a certain sort of identity is proclaimed incessantly as the norm. The imperatives of marketing and advertising have created stories which speak to us directly, flatter us, deceive us into believing the world is here because it owes us something. Every message that speaks to us directly as 'you' is aiming to do that. It may be ironic, but the aim of this 'you' is the 'I'. You must buy this iPod. You must shoot this film on your iPhone and put it on YouTube. It's flattery, and it's pleasing, at some level. But it is only a moment of interface between the meaning and experience of our lives and the broader unfathomable vortex of global complexity in which our lives are increasingly caught up—its economics, its politics, its tides of ecological and cultural toxins. Yet, against this sort of 'you' there is another identity which we still have—that of our films. Indian cinema at some fundamental level revels in the rather non-modern idea that we are not the centre of the world. It values the recognition of the existence of others over the inflation of delusions of the narcissistic self. In some ways, perhaps that is why we have both the world's biggest democracy and the world's biggest film industry. *Could we have a democracy if we did not feel—as a profound truth somewhere deep inside us—the fact that others live as well?* In our lives and in our films, we do not ever presume to doubt the right of the other to exist, the way modernity's excessive arrogance has caused so many to do, including the modern fundamentalist who claims to be against modernity. In celebrating belonging, being for others, our films lift the uncertainty off our own selves that inevitably comes from self-primacy. They give us a sort of emotional shelter that the modern world scarcely can.

We are, in the general narrative world of our films, experiencing the cultural expression of one of the last vestiges of humanism in a world which has twisted itself into a state far beyond our understanding. When we watch, we forget

not just our specific problems of families or work, of sociology
or economics, but really a way of living in the world that has
become the norm under modernity. What we forget, when
we lose ourselves in the joys and sorrows of our films, is the
burden of the modern self itself. In our films, we feel what it's
like not just to be someone else but really, to be *someone
else's*—and not in a carnal way, not in the least. We feel
belonging. We feel what it is to have someone to live for—
parents, children, spouses, friends—all the things which still
exist in real life under modernity, but simply do not enjoy the
primacy or role they once did in our culture's stories about
itself. Indian cinema is our antidote to modernity, even as it
exists very much within it. In our films, we become an 'I' that
only says 'you'. It is the sense of the 'you' that appears as the
moment of closure in *Hum Aapke Hain Koun..!* when the
'koun' drops off, leaving us with one elevating proclamation:
Hum aapke hain. We are yours. In its largest sense, it is the
'you' that the child-saint Bhakta Prahlada sings to and sings
of in the old AVM classic. 'Jeevamu neeve katha?' he asks.
'Aren't You Life itself?' This 'You' was Lord Vishnu for him,
but in the countless tales of our films and our lives, it could
be anyone—Allah, Yesu, Khwaja, Guru, Maa, Amma, Nanna,
Son, Daughter, Brother, Sister, Friend, you. 'You' are not
what a worldwide outbreak of mass-mediated greed, cruelty
and selfishness says you are. You are Life, simply, being lived
through you.

ACKNOWLEDGEMENTS

I WOULD LIKE TO ACKNOWLEDGE MY MOTHER'S HELP IN MY RESEARCH for at least one part of this book. The first chapter, 'God', draws on interviews I did with some of her colleagues from the Telugu and Tamil film industries on the subject of mythological cinema, a topic that has been of particular interest for me given the recent debates and controversies about religion and media. For this incredible access, I thank her. And for their graciousness and time, I thank Mr Bapu, the legendary artist and perhaps the greatest living myth-maker of Telugu cinema; his respected writer-collaborator, the late Mr Mullapudi Ramana; the late Mr Gummadi Venkateshwar Rao; the late Mr Kanta Rao; Ms Laya; the late Mr M.S. Reddy; Ms Roja Ramani and Mr Saravanan of the venerable house of AVM. I would also like to thank the director and staff of the National Film Archives of India, Pune, for their help and support for my research on the subject.

I am equally grateful to the people in the place that has given me my way of seeing the world of our films—my students and colleagues at the University of San Francisco (USF). I would like to thank, in particular, the students of the 'Understanding India' and 'Indian Cinema' courses, and salute, in particular, our team of self-professed 'Gandhian gangsters'—Conor Rowley, Nick Milo, Kate Ory, Peter Flores, Raquel Martinez, Kate Viernes, Charlie Ainslee and Natasha Pietruschka, whose trip for a summer class in Hyderabad turned out to be one of the most fulfilling experiences of my teaching career. The attempt to understand India and its cinema in the most universal, relevant way possible for them brought me to this particular way of telling the story.

Also at the University of San Francisco, I thank Shalendra Sharma, for his strong encouragement and support on my scholarship. I acknowledge with gratitude and appreciation my friends and colleagues Elliot Neaman, Andrew Goodwin, John Nelson, Vijaya Nagarajan, Lois Lorentzen, Marco Jacquemet, Chris Kamrath, Dean Rader, Jeff Paris, Julio Moreno, Uldis Kruze, Scott Nunes, Peter Novak, Rhonda McGee, Elena Flores, Susan Paik and Brandon Brown. I thank the Faculty Development Fund and John Pinelli for making my numerous research trips possible. I would also like to thank Sharon Li and Liza Locsin for all their support, and extend an especially loud round of applause and adulation for the media studies department's inimitable Lydia Fedulow. Also, at USF, I would like to thank for their support for the 'India' programme and classes former Dean Stanley Nel, who got me started on it; Vice Provost Gerardo Marin, who brought it to fruition and Provost Jennifer Turpin, who has been a pillar of support for matters of truth and justice. Finally, I salute, as always, Father Steve Privett, who, among many other things, was gracious enough to visit my 'Understanding India' class and share his thoughts on his India visit.

In India, I would like to thank the University of Hyderabad (UoH), for calling me a 'friend of the programme', and I do my best to be one. It has been a second home for me over the years, and I thank UNESCO Professor Vinod Pavarala and Aparna Rayaprol for helping me put the USF-UoH programme together, and for welcoming my students so warmly. For their hospitality and their constant research support, I thank former V.C. B.P. Sanjay, Probal Dasgupta, Kanchan, Thirumal and the staff of the Study in India Program. I reserve an especially affectionate and appreciative thank-you for UoH's finest, and my students' local guide and compadre, the amazing 'Bugs' Bhargav.

I would also like to thank the entire team that worked on this book at Penguin Books India, and add a special round of thanks to Udayan Mitra and Ambar Sahil Chatterjee for ensuring its timely arrival to celebrate this auspicious centenary year of Indian cinema.

Finally, I would like to thank those who have believed in my writing and me without telling the two apart—it is a great help. Carl Bromley remains a source of enthusiasm and support for all things to do with Indian cinema. Anand Kamalakar is no fan of the frivolous stuff, but a man of cinema, and good friend too. Long overdue debts to my uncle Mr B.P.R. Vithal, for reality checks on all matters driven by the intellectual impulse; to Mrs Seshu Vithal; and to Nivedita and S.M. Kumar for the enduring over-the-wall bond. No book I ever write can fail to hail Dr Sanjaya Baru and Dr Rama Baru for years of friendship and support. Lakshmi Attha remains a source of spirit and strength, from near or far. I also thank Ravikanth Sabnavis and Rajnikanth Sabnavis for much support over the years on pursuing my writing interests. My sister Sravanthi helped tremendously when the class came to Hyderabad, and she is duly and affectionately acknowledged, and so is Cousin Kusu. The greatest thanks are also due for this book and more to Dr V. Sadanand and Smt. Mridula. My stays in Pune and all the hospitality were joyously provided by my bavagaru and the tallest among the new generation of myth-munis, Vikram Veturi. Thanks also to Shekhar and Sheetal Mondkar–Veturi for years of affection and support. Almost the last, but certainly not the least, all manner of thanks to Lakshmi, for inspiration, example and friendship, and for having two of me now to deal with, as you put it—the newest being my son, Varenya, who shakes up my laptop and makes me believe he will do that to whatever remains wrong in this world too. At last, I thank, most of all, my father, Professor J.V. Ramana Rao, and my mother, Smt. Jamuna, the People's Actress.

REFERENCES

Ahmad, A. (1992). Bombay films: The cinema as metaphor for Indian society and politics. *Modern Asian Studies*, 26, 289-320.

Anderson, B. (1991). *Imagined communities: Reflections on the origin and spread of nationalism*. London: Verso Books.

Babb, L. & Wadley, S. (Eds.). (1995). *Media and the transformation of religion in South Asia*. Philadelphia: University of Pennsylvania Press.

Badrinath, C. (2006). *The Mahabharata: An inquiry in the human condition*. Hyderabad: Orient Longman India.

Bajaj, V. (11 February 2007). In India the golden age of television is now. *New York Times*. Retrieved from http://www.nytimes.com.

Bakshi, R. (1998). Raj Kapoor: From Jis Desh Mein Ganga Behti Hain to Ram Teri Ganga Maili. In A. Nandy (Ed.). *The secret politics of our desires: Innocence, culpability and Indian popular cinema* (pp. 92–133). New Delhi: Oxford University Press.

Balagopal, K. (1995). Politics as property. *Economic and Political Weekly, XXX* (40), pp. 2482–84.

Bijapurkar, R. (4 March 1998). A market in discontinuity. *Economic Times*.

Brosius, C. (2005). The scattered homelands of the migrant: Bollyworld through the diasporic lens. In R. Kaur & A. Sinha (Eds.). *Bollyworld: Popular Indian cinema through a transnational lens* (pp. 207–238). New Delhi: Sage.

Butcher, M. (1997). Looking at Ms. World. *Seminar*, 453, 16–20.

Chakravarty, S. (1993). *National identity in Indian popular cinema 1947–87*. Austin, TX: University of Texas Press.

Das Gupta, C. (1989). Seeing and believing, science and religion: Notes on the 'mythological' genre. *Film Quarterly*, 42, 12–18.

Das Gupta, C. (2008). *Seeing is believing: Selected writings on cinema*. New Delhi: Viking/Penguin.

Dehejia, H. (2003). Introduction: Evam Saundaryam. *Evam: Forum on Indian representations*, 2, 1–10.

Deshpande, S. (2005). The consumable hero of globalized India. In R. Kaur & A. Sinha (Eds.). *Bollyworld: Popular Indian cinema through a transnational lens* (pp. 186–203). New Delhi: Sage.

Dickey, S. (1993). *Cinema and the urban poor in South India*. Cambridge: Cambridge University Press.

Dickey, S. (1996). Consuming utopia: Film watching in Tamil Nadu. In C. Breckenridge (Ed.). Consuming modernity: Public culture in India (pp. 131–56). Minneapolis: University of Minnesota Press.

Dirks, N. (2001). The home and the nation: Consuming culture and politics in *Roja*. In R. Dwyer & C. Pinney (Eds.). *Pleasure and the nation: The history, politics, and consumption of public culture in India* (pp. 161–185) New Delhi: Oxford University Press.

Dudrah, R. (2002). Vilayati Bollywood: Popular Hindi cinema-going and diasporic South Asian identity in Birmingham (UK). *The Public*, 9, 19–36.

Dwyer, R. (2006). *Filming the gods: Religion in Indian cinema*. New York: Routledge.

Dwyer, R. & Patel, D. (2002). *Cinema India: The visual culture of Hindi film*. London: Reaktion Books.

Eck, D. (1981). *Darsan: Seeing the divine image in India*. New York: Columbia University Press.

Fernandes, L. (2006). *India's new middle class: Democratic politics in an era of economic reform*. Minneapolis: University of Minnesota Press.

Gahlaut, K. (31 January 2005). The yippie generation. *India Today*, pp. 6–9.

Ganti, T. (2004). *Bollywood: A guidebook to popular Hindi cinema.* New York: Routledge.

Guha, R. (2007). *India after Gandhi: The history of the world's largest democracy.* New York: HarperCollins.

Gummadi, V. (2006). Personal interview.

Harak, S. (2000). Afterword. In S. Harak (ed.), *Nonviolence for third millennium* (pp. 229–34). Macon, GA: Mercer University Press.

Hughes, S. (2005). Mythologicals and modernity: Contesting silent cinema in South India. *PostScripts, 1.2/1.3,* 207–35.

Huntington, S. (1993). The clash of civilizations? *Foreign Affairs,* 3, pp. 22–49.

Hussain, S. (6–12 August 1997). V'Jaying on. *The Economic Times,* p. 8.

Jeffrey, R. (1997). Telugu: Ingredients of growth and failure. *Economic and Political Weekly, XXXII* (5), pp. 192–95.

Jhally, S. & Lewis, J. (1992). *Enlightened racism: The Cosby Show, audiences, and the myth of the American dream.* Boulder, CO: Westview Press.

Joseph, M. (6 November 2000). Riverdale sonata. *Outlook.* Retrieved from http://www.outlookindia.com on 30 December 2004.

Juluri, V. (1999). Global weds local: The reception of *Hum Aapke Hain Koun. European Journal of Cultural Studies,* 2, 231–248.

Juluri, V. (2003). *Becoming a global audience: Longing and belonging in Indian music television.* New York: Peter Lang.

Kaviraj, S. (1992). The imaginary institution of India. In P. Chatterjee & G. Pande (Eds.). *Subaltern studies 7: Writings on South Asian history and society* (pp. 1–39). New Delhi: Oxford University Press.

Kaviraj, S. (1998). The culture of representative democracy. In P. Chatterjee (Ed.). *Wages of freedom: Fifty years of the Indian nation state* (pp. 147–175). New Delhi: Oxford University Press.

Kazmi, F. (1998). How angry is the angry young man? 'Rebellion' in conventional Hindi films. In A. Nandy (Ed.). *The secret politics of our desires: Innocence, culpability and Indian popular cinema* (pp. 134–55). New Delhi: Oxford University Press.

Khilnani, S. (1999). *The idea of India*. New York: Farrar Strauss Giroux.

Khilnani, S. (31 January 2005). The bubble syndrome. *India Today*, pp. 16–17.

Kohli, V. (2003). *The Indian media business*. New Delhi: Sage.

Kumar, S. (2006). *Gandhi meets primetime: Globalization and nationalism in Indian television*. Chicago: University of Illinois Press.

Luce, H. (2007). *In spite of the gods: The strange rise of modern India*. New York: Random House.

Lynch, O. (1990). The social construction of emotion in India. In O. Lynch (Ed.). *The social construction of emotion in India* (pp. 3–34). Berkeley: University of California Press.

Mankekar, P. (1999). *Screening culture, viewing politics: An ethnography of television, womanhood and nation in postcolonial India*. Durham: Duke University Press.

Mattelart, A. (1994). *Mapping world communication: War, progress, culture* (S. Emmanuel & J. Cohen, trans.). Minneapolis: University of Minnesota.

Mazzarella, W. (2003). *Shoveling smoke: Advertising and globalization in contemporary India*. New Delhi: Oxford University Press.

McCaughan, D. (4–10 March 1998). Hanging out? That's cool! *The Economic Times*.

Mehta, S. (2004). *Maximum city: Bombay lost and found*. New York: Knopf.

Monteiro, A. (1998). Official television and the unofficial fabrications of the self: The spectator as subject. In A. Nandy (Ed). *The secret politics of our desires: Innocence, culpability and Indian popular cinema* (pp. 157–207). New Delhi: Oxford University Press.

Naipaul, V.S. (18 August 1997) A million mutinies. *India Today*, pp. 36–39.

Nandy, A. (1987) From outside the imperium: Gandhi's cultural critique of the West. In A. Nandy (Ed.). *Traditions, tyrannies and utopias: Essays in the politics of awareness* (pp. 127–62). New Delhi: Oxford University Press.

Nandy, A. (2001). *An ambiguous journey to the city: The village and other odd ruins of the self in the Indian imagination*. New Delhi: Oxford University Press.

Neuss, J. (1998). The NTR phenomenon reconsidered. Originally published in *Internationales Asienforum*, 1–2, 23–45.

Niranjana, T. & Srinivas, S.V. (1996), Managing the crisis: Bharateeyudu and the ambivalence of being Indian. *Economic and Political Weekly, XXXI* (48), pp. 3129–34.

Paranjape, M. (2003). Foreword. *Evam: Forum on Indian representations*, 2, i–ix.

Parekh, B. (2001) *Gandhi: A very short introduction*. Oxford: Oxford University Press.

Pattanaik, D. (2006). *Myth = mithya: A handbook of Hindu mythology*. New Delhi: Penguin Books India.

Pinto, J. (2006). *Helen: The life and times of a H-bomb*. New Delhi: Penguin Books India.

Rajadhyaksha, A. & Willemen, P. (1999). *Encyclopedia of Indian cinema*. New Delhi: Oxford University Press.

Rajagopal, A. (2001). *Politics after television: Hindu nationalism and the reshaping of the public in India*. Cambridge: Cambridge University Press.

Ramana, M. (2006, June). Personal interview.

Rao, K. (2006, July). Personal interview.

Reddy, M. S. (2006, August). Personal interview.

Roberts, P. (1996). *Empire of the soul: Some journeys in India*. New York: Riverhead Books.

Rowell, L. (1992). *Music and musical thought in ancient India*. Chicago: University of Chicago Press.

Shah, A. (1997). *Hype, hypocricy and television in urban India*. New Delhi: Vikas.

Sharma, A. (2000). *Classical Hindu thought: An introduction*. New Delhi: Oxford University Press.

Singh, K. (2003). Preface: Satyam. Shivam, Sundaram. *Evam: Forum on Indian representations, 2*, x–xi.

Srinivas, S. V. (2001). Telugu folklore films: The case of Paatala Bhairavi. *Deep Focus: A Film Quarterly, 9* (1), 45–50.

Srinivas, S. V. (1996). Devotion and defiance in fan activity. *Journal of Arts and Ideas*, 29, 67–83.

Talk-a-Tone. (1944). Films and post-war era. Volume 8, Number 3, pp. 7–10.

Tharoor, S. (15 August 2003). A land governed by film stars. *New York Times*.

Uberoi, P. (2001). Imagining the family: An ethnography of viewing *Hum Aapke Hain Koun*. In R. Dwyer & C. Pinney (Eds.) *Pleasure and the nation: The history, politics, and consumption of public culture in India* (pp. 309–51). New Delhi: Oxford University Press.

Vachani, L. (1999). Bachchan-alias: The many faces of a film icon. In C. Brosius & M. Butcher (Eds.). *Image journeys: Audio-visual media and cultural change in India* (pp. 199–230). New Delhi: Sage.

Vaidyanathan, T.G. (1989). Authority and identity in India. *Daedalus, 118*, 147–69.

Varma, P. (2004). *Being Indian: The truth about why the 21st century will be India's*. New Delhi: Penguin Books India.

Vasudevan, R. (2001). Bombay and its public. In R. Dwyer & C. Pinney (Eds). *Pleasure and the nation: The history, politics, and consumption of public culture in India* (pp. 186–211). New Delhi: Oxford University Press.

INDEX

Adavi Ramudu (1977), 107

Advani, L.K., 129

Ahmad, Akbar, 63

Amar Akbar Anthony (1977), 80, 86, 171

Amar Chitra Katha, 15

Ambedkar, B.R., 43, 57

Ammoru (1995), 45

Anderson, Benedict, 58

Anjaiah, T., 110–11

Annamayya (1997), 46

Anniyan (2005), 169

Anukokunda Oka Roju (Unexpectedly one day, 2005), 190–91

Aparachitudu (2005), 167, 169

Ashok Kumar, 123

Austin Powers (1997), 170

AVM Productions, 165, 196, 197

Awara (1951), 71–72

Ayodhya Ka Raja (1932), 31

Baapu Cheppina Maata (What Bapu told us, 2005), 176

Bachchan, Amitabh, 11, 60, 64, 76, 79–81, 158, 167, 194

Bala Ramayanam (1997), 33

Bapu, 25, 34, 197

Baywatch, 134, 141–42

Benegal, Shyam, 176

Bhagavad Gita, 36–37, 50–51

Bhakta Vidur (1921), 18, 59

Bharateeyudu (Indian, 1996), 167–68, 182

Bhukailasa (1940), 22, 65, 107

Birth of Shri Krishna, The (1920), 39

Bold and the Beautiful, The, 141

Bombay (1995), 167, 171

Bose, Subhas Chandra, 168

Brook, Peter, 31, 126

Buniyaad (beginning 1986), 101

Channel V, 135, 148, 149–52

Chattopadhyay, Sarat Chandra, 62

Children of Men (2006), 189

Chinai, Alisha, 147–53

Chiranjeevi, 167

Chitrahaar, 97

Chopra, Deepak, 48

Circus Ramudu (1980), 107

Company (2002), 135, 167, 173–74

Cosmos, 139

Da Vinci Code, The (2006), 17

Dallas, 139

Dana Veera Shura Karna(1977), 74, 107–08

Darr (1993), 167

Das Gupta, Chidananda, 16, 33, 40

Deewar (1975), 79–80

Devdas (1935), 60, 62–64, 69, 82

Dilwale Dulhania Le Jayenge (DDLJ, 1995), 158

Discovery of India, 123

Don (1978), 79, 81

Doordarshan, 96–104, 112, 114–15, 119, 121-22, 127, 139-40, 142, 144, 149, 150

Draupadi Vastrapaharanam, 32

Dutt, Nargis, 70

Dwyer, Rachel, 8, 17, 22, 31, 33, 41, 42, 43, 44, 45, 96

Eenadu (newspaper), 109

Eenadu Television, 34, 148

Ek Anekaur Ekta, 122

El TV, 144

Films Division, 102, 122

Gandhi, Indira, 67, 73, 74, 75, 95, 98, 110, 112, 117, 119, 138

Gandhi, M.K., 8, 18, 19, 37, 43–44, 57, 59, 63–65, 66, 68, 71, 72-73, 75, 81, 85, 93–95, 116, 135, 136, 164, 168, 174–89, 191, 194

Gandhi, My Father (2007), 176

Gandhi, Rajiv, 110-11, 119, 128–29

Haasan, Kamal, 167, 169

Harak, Simon, 178

Harishchandrachi Factory (2009), 192–93

Helen, 138

Hughes, Stephen, 29, 59

Hum Aapke Hain Koun (HAHK), 96, 135, 154–58, 165, 196

Hum Log (beginning 1984), 100–01, 103

Hyderabad Blues (1998), 164-65

IMAX, 3

Indian, 167

'Jago Mohan Pyare', 70

Jagte Raho (1956), 69–70

Jain TV, 144

Jamuna, 33, 200

'Jeevamuneevekatha', 196

Jis Desh Mein Ganga Behti Hai (1960), 72–73

Kaante (2002), 185
Kapoor, Raj, 11, 60, 68–72, 86, 138, 158, 194
Kapur, Shekhar, 104
Khadgam (Dagger, 2002), 172
Khan, Shah Rukh (SRK), 158, 160, 165
Khandaan (beginning 1985), 101
Khanna, Rajesh, 75
Krishna Deva Raya, King of Vijayanagara, 112
Kuch Kuch Hota Hai (1998), 135, 160
Kukunoor, Nagesh, 164-65

Laden, Osama bin, 172
Lagaan (2001), 162
Lage Raho Munna Bhai (2006), 135, 174–94
Lakshya (2004), 162
Lava Kusha (1963), 36
Lucy Show, The, 97, 139

Macaulay, Thomas Babington, 58
'Made in India', 147–53
Mahabharat (serial), 11, 15, 127
Mahabharata, 26, 27, 31, 38, 74, 114, 126
Maine Gandhi Ko Nahin Mara (2005), 176
Making of Mahatma, The (1996), 176

Mana Desam (Our nation, 1949), 65
Manoj Kumar, 138
Masoom (1983), 104
Maya Bazar (1956), 26-27, 28, 36, 45, 107
'Mere Desh Ki Dharti', 68
Mille, Cecil B. De, 16
Mission Kashmir (2000), 8, 135, 167, 172–73
Mother India (1957), 61, 68
Mr India (1987), 172
MTV, 135,140, 141, 148, 150, 151, 155, 158-59, 163, 194
Munna Bhai M.B.B.S. (2003), 174-75
Muqaddar ka Sikandar (1978), 81
Musharraf, Pervez, 172

Nagaiah, Chittooru, 23
Naz Cinema, 185-87
Nehru, Jawaharlal, 8, 11, 57, 60, 66–68, 71, 72, 73, 75, 85, 91, 93–95, 96, 98, 105, 109, 116, 117, 136–38, 164, 168

Om Shanti Om (2007), 190

Paalu Chelu, 97
Padamati Sandhya Ragam (The West's song of dusk, 1987), 139

Pardes (197), 158
Parekh, Bhikhu, 43, 187–88
Parinda (1989), 173
Parsi Theatre, 18
Patala Bhairavi (1951), 107
Patel, Vallabhbhai, 57
Pattanaik, Devdutt, 21
Peepli (Live) (2010), 192
Phalke, Dundiraj Govind, 16, 18, 39–40, 59, 193
'Piya Bin', 62
Prabhat, 44

Raghavendra Swamy, 34
Rahman, A.R., 146, 171
Raja Harischandra (1913), 10, 59, 61, 192, 193
Rajinikanth, 165, 167
Ramachandran, M.G. (MGR), 106
Ramana, Mullapudi, 25–26, 37, 197
Ramayan (serial), 11, 15, 39–40, 45, 92, 114–28, 129
Ramayana, 30, 114, 117, 120, 122-23, 124, 125, 126
Ramoji Film City, 3
Ranade, Mahadev Govind, 44
Rang De Basanti, 167
Rao, Akkineni Nageswara, 27
Rao, Gummadi Venkateshwar, 27, 32, 197
Rao, Kanta, 33, 35, 197

Rao, N.T. Rama (NTR), 11, 26-27, 33, 65, 74, 92, 105, 104–14, 118, 128
Rao, P.V. Narasimha, 140
Rao, S.V. Ranga, 27, 33
Ray, Satyajit, 82
Reagan, Ronald, 106
Reddy, M.S., 30, 32, 33, 197
Reservoir Dogs, 185
Rising, The, 167
Roja, 167, 170–71
Roshan, Hrithik, 162, 172–73

Sagan, Carl, 139
Sagar, Ramanand, 122
Saigal, K.L., 62–63
Sampoorna Ramayanam (1936), 32
Sant Tukaram (1936), 18, 23
Santa Barbara, 144
Satya (1998), 169, 175
Savitri, 27
Scarface, 176
Shankar, 167-169
Shiva (1989), 166–67
Sholay (1975), 76–77, 79
Shree 420 (1955), 70
Shri Krishna Tulabharam (1966), 27-28
Shri Krishnarjuna Yuddham (1962), 27-28
Singh, Dara, 34
Singh, V.P., 117-18, 129

Sivaji (2007), 165
Sri Ramadasu (2006), 46
Sriramulu, Potti, 93
Star Trek, 139
Star TV, 134-35, 140-41, 143, 147, 148
Subah (beginning 1987), 101–02
Superman (1980), 107
Surabhi, 18
Swades (2004), 165

Taare Zameen Par (2007), 186
Tamas (1986), 101
Telugu Desam Party (TDP), 108, 111, 113-14
Tharoor, Shashi, 105
Top of the Pops, 139
Tyagayya (1946), 18, 23
Tyagayya (the Saint), 23, 194

Udham Singh, 149
Upkar (1967), 68

Vemana, 112
Verma, Ram Gopal, 166
Vetagadu (1979), 107

World This Week, The, 139

Yeh Jo Hai Zindagi (beginning 1984), 102

Zanjeer (1973), 76
Zee TV, 140